EVANGELISM THAT DECOLONIZES THE SOUL

Partnership With Christ

BISHOP ABEL TENDEKAYI MUZOREWA, M.A., D.D.

Eugene, Oregon

**EVANGELISM THAT
DECOLONIZES THE SOUL**

*Copyright © 2005 by Bishop Abel Tendekayi Muzorewa,
P O Box BW 353, Borrowdale, Zimbabwe.*

ISBN: 1-59752-445-X

Wipf and Stock Publishers
199 West 8th Avenue
Eugene OR 97401

www.wipfandstock.com

No part of this work may be reproduced or transmitted in any form or by any means, electronic or mechanical, including photocopying and recording, or by any information storage or retrieval system, except as may be expressly permitted by the author in writing or his assigns in writing. Requests for permission should be addressed to the author.

DEDICATION

This book is dedicated to:

Adored late grandmother, Maitirwa Dorcas (Mafarachisi) Munangatire, who raised me with love and charity from two years of age to nine, and her husband Grandpa Abraham Munangatire,

Beloved late parents: Haadi Philemon Muzorewa, father, grandpa, pastor/teacher, successful farmer and musician and Takaruda Hilda (Munangatire) Muzorewa, most exemplary and ideal Christian mother, a prayer warrior and a distinctive church choir soprano,
and
Cherished late Rev. Josiah Chimbadzwa, my homiletics lecturer and marriage officer, who was preaching an evangelistic sermon, including an altar call the day I was born again.

TABLE OF CONTENTS

ACKNOWLEDGEMENTS vii

INTRODUCTION ix

1: HOW I BECAME A CHRISTIAN
    I.   My Humble Faith Journey 1
    II. Accepting Christ Personally................ 4

2: THE GOSPEL IMPERATIVE
    I.   The Harvest is Ripe 9
    II. God's Love 11
    III. The Need for Salvation/Wholeness 14
    IV. Salvation is Available 15
    V. Transformation of the Human Condition 17
    VI. The Liberation of the Oppressed 19
    VII. Humanity's Yearning for Eternity 24

3: THE CORNERSTONE OF EVANGELISM
    I.   God in African Traditional Religion 27
    II. The Bible 29
    III. The Risen Christ 32
    IV. The Holy Spirit: 39
    V. Culture: Inculturation 45
    VI. Christian Experience 48

4: EVANGLISM THAT DECOLONIZES THE SOUL
    I.   What Evangelism is Not 51
    II. Defining Evangelism that Decolonizes
         the Soul 52

5: INSTRUMENTS AND MEANS OF EVANGELISM
    I.   The Power of Prayer 59
    II. The Power of the Sermon 66
    III. The Power of Living Personal Testimonies 67
    IV. Power in Music! 68
    V. Planning Evangelistic Music Service 70

6: EVANGELISM THAT PRODUCES DEFINITE RESULTS
    I.   Personal Evangelism Method 73
    II. Situational Evangelism .... 83.
    III. The Fishing Goes On 91

7: THE PASTOR IS KEY
    I.   Cases in Point 99
    II. Where Did We Go Wrong 102
    III. Resurrecting a Dying Congregation 106
    IV. Six Traits of an Evangelistic Preacher. 110
    V. Preparation of an Evangelistic Sermon 114
    VI. Hope for Universal Revitalization 119
    VII. A New 21st Century Message is Due 120

A PRAYER FOR AFRICA 125

APPENDIX 1: STATISTICS 129

BIBLIOGRAPHY 131

ACKNOWLEDGEMENTS

First, I acknowledge God who created me and protected me from the dangers of being born prematurely and from cruelty of society as you will learn in chapter ONE.

Next, I wish to thank my wife Maggie for all her prayerful support throughout my ministry, evangelism and during the writing of this book; whether together or apart in Borrowdale, Houston, London and Pennsylvania, I was mindful of your presence.

The day I actually started writing this book I was a guest for two weeks in the Washington DC home of The Rev. Cecil Mudede and his family. I continued working flat out at the Houston home of our dearest and only daughter Charity, who is always both my personal nurse and secretary.

I am indebted to my caring brother, Gwinyai, whose editorial assistance brought this book into existence. I also thank my sister-in-law, Susan, whose generous hospitality is greatly appreciated. My brother Farai David weighed-in with his sharp insights and my oldest son, Tendekai Blessing joined me there just when I needed his computer proficiency to 'cut and paste,' the manuscript -- a true *blessing*. His brother, Tanyaradzwa Wesley who contributed his journalistic skills in developing the manuscript. I thank them all for their immeasurable moral support, assistance and contribution to the titling process.

I also thank Mr. Tafadzwa Mudambanuki (UMCOM) for furnishing certain factual data. Nancy Wiegel and Janice Fay-Walker, respectively a Religion Major and Department Secretary at Lincoln University, PA, helped to type and give the manuscript its presentable form.

My other brothers, their spouses, my nephews, niece and son, each in their special way have contributed to transferring this book from mental pages to paper pages; Basil Chenjerai, Ernest Irimayi, Gwinyai Paidamoyo, Kudzai Haadi, and Chipo Hilda.

Words are not enough to thank Bishop Eben K. Nhiwatiwa. His spirituality has always blessed me long before he was elected bishop: the support of the conferences of his Zimbabwe Area in launching the Bishop A. T. Muzorewa Evangelism Foundation is tremendously appreciated, as is the use of excerpts on *1918 Holy Spirit* from his book 'Humble Beginnings'. I appreciate my immediate successor Bishop Christopher Jokomo's practice of making altar calls -- even at funerals. This led me to unearth some interesting history of the invitational system in Chapter 6.

I thank Rev. Fanuel Kadenge, my best friend under the sun, who props me up spiritually when the going is rough for use of the 'conversion on the bus' story in Chapter 5; Rev. Dr. Isaac Mawokomatanda, his wife Ruth, my niece Wendy Mhlanga, her brother Lazarus and his wife Maggie Mhlanga whose generous monetary gifts I used to sustain the project.

I would be remiss if I do not express my gratitude to a committee set up to pray for this project as well as the ATME Foundation; they are the Reverends P. Mupindu, F. Nyagato, F. Kadenge, K. Kahlari, S. Tapfuma, Mai Rudo Bingepinge, Mai Tabitha Katsande and my daughter-in-law, Mai Chikanhwa Florence Muzorewa -- an inspirational evangelistic preacher as she itinerates all over Zimbabwe. May God continue to bless all these 'Prayer Warriors' and kind hearts for their love and caring during what turned out to be a rather stressful duration.

Finally, I also acknowledge a former missionary to Zimbabwe, the late M.J. Muphree from Oneanta, Alabama, USA -- who was an evangelist at heart. He taught me practical evangelism and winning souls for Christ. He gave me a firm foundation when I served as his Assistant Conference Director of Evangelism in Zimbabwe.

Of course, I take responsibility for all the errors in this book. I also welcome any comments.

I remain,
One with many to thank,
                    ... much to be grateful for. ††

INTRODUCTION

> *"After this, the Lord appointed seventy-two others and sent them two-by-two ahead of him to every town and place where he was about to go. He told them, "The harvest is plentiful, but the workers are few. Ask the Lord of the harvest, therefore, to send out workers into his harvest field. "Go! I am sending you out like lambs among wolves." (Luke 10, 1-3).*

This book is a result of what I believe is divine inspiration triggered in my soul by Jesus' words: 'The harvest is plentiful, but the workers are few." (Luke 10:2). The concept of sending and being sent also struck another note -- "obedience": "Peace be with you! As the father has sent me, I am sending you." (John 20:21). Before I accepted this task to share the vision with my fellow Christians who may read this book, I had to offer an agonizing prayer and invite others to pray for me and with me so that I might be obedient to the Lord in writing this book.

Additionally, I believe that God inspired me to write this book on this particular subject because God knows where my heart is -- in respect to Africa and how I feel when I see crowds of people in need of salvation. The challenge was that it was not enough just to "cry for my beloved country" but I had to proactively tackle the task of evangelising the unchurched of the land. Please note that this book is not an attempt to try new evangelistic methods, or a theology of evangelism, or a contemporary theory. I leave these for others to work on. Rather we have here Practical Evangelism -- a simple but clear message to those desiring to present the simple gospel not only to " the least of these my brothers and sisters" (Matthew 25:40) but to the powers that be. Thus, if you are a person who is filled with a deep desire and passion for:

- ➢ the presence of the Christ of faith;
- ➢ winning people to this Christ so that they may grow to be faithful, effective servants of Jesus and the church may grow fast;
- ➢ returning spiritual vitality in the main line denominations; i.e. reversing the present declining trend to growth spirit;
- ➢ being Christ's agent, not spectator, and
- ➢ spiritual self-revival;

then **this is the book that reveals how and equips you to make a difference for Christ**.

Furthermore, this book is intended to stimulate and enrich one's devotional needs, through illustrations that assist a believer to realize that the risen Lord, the Christ of faith, the Saviour of experience is here, there and everywhere.

If the accounts shared in this book strike the reader as "unreal", it is because the modern day person tends to be more comfortable "walking by sight" not by the Biblical faith. The invitation extended in this book is that we "walk by faith, not by sight" because the subject is the Christ of faith. This book clearly *disproves the theory that miracles are a thing of the past.*

For those individual lay and clergy people who have a desire to be holy, and win others for Christ, this is your book. I believe Christ is calling lay people through this book to lead others to the abundant life, which he gives.[Luke 10:1-3] The sole credential needed is obedience to the gospel imperative. (Matthew 28:19-20)

For the lay evangelists and clergy evangelists who really mean business, i.e. those who truly and deeply desire to win people for Christ and bring them to church, keep them interested in doing the Lord's work, you are blessed already because you are in partnership with Christ who is victorious. **The only secret is, after reading this book, practice what it advocates!**

Briefly, let me walk you through the book:

Chapter One: How I became a Christian, shares with the reader what the grace of God has done for me without an iota of merit on my part. I don't deserve His grace, yet God intentionally chose me to be *His vassal*. Indeed my life is a manifestation of the hand of mercy tested so far for 80 years.

Chapter Two: Gospel Imperative, places emphasis on preaching the gospel in Africa *now*. What is the urgency? What is the ideal time to obey Christ? Is now too early to obey the Lord?

Chapter Three: The Cornerstone of Evangelism lays the foundation for the type of evangelism that decolonizes the person. This is a four-fold cornerstone: God, the Bible, the Risen Christ and the Holy Spirit. We show that *Jesus and the Holy Spirit are neither museum or archives items nor just one more academic subject of discussion.*

Chapter Four: Evangelism that Decolonizes the Soul, by God's grace, attempts to clearly define evangelism as I experienced it and as I observed what the gospel has done in our midst.

Chapter Five: The Instruments and Means of Evangelism, presents us with the means. Just as any craftsman must have appropriate tools to do their work efficiently and successfully, this chapter suggests the more appropriate tools to "do the work of an evangelist." (II Tim 4:5). The clue here is practicing, not just theory.

Chapter Six: Evangelism that Produces Definite Results, is supreme for those who are in interested in more than just debates, dissertations, and short arguments about evangelism. It is for those who intend to obey Jesus -- honestly and faithfully obey Jesus: "TO MAKE DISCIPLES." With this message and method they cannot fail. **Winning persons to Christ through personal evangelism is the**

supreme method that truly works.

Chapter Seven: The Pastor is Key, is a challenge to all who claim that they were called by God to leave all other careers to be shepherds of His people. In my opinion, this chapter lays a fair burden of shepherding squarely on the pastor. Revitalizing the congregation helps us to resurrect the church. I contend that the pastor holds the key to either lock or unlock the death or resurrection doors for the congregation. -- yes, the whole church.

Now, therefore, proceed to prayerfully read, study and apply the spirit and content of the book. And may the grace of our Lord Jesus Christ be with you - Amen. †††

One
HOW I BECAME A CHRISTIAN

I. MY HUMBLE FAITH JOURNEY BY THE GRACE OF GOD

The God of Africa is the same God who is the father of our Lord Jesus Christ. I believe that this is the God who has poured His Spirit upon me from the time I was in my mother's womb, and called me to the ministry, just like He did upon Jeremiah. *"Before I formed you in the womb I knew you, before you were born I set you apart, I appointed you to the nations."* (Jer. 1:5)

With these words I want to welcome you Dear Reader to my faith journey, and to what God called me to do. Before we share thoughts on evangelism that decolonizes the soul, I wish to acquaint the reader with my life journey so far. But a word of caution first: although this is my life's journey, I will often use the possessive pronouns "we" and "our" because, as an African we use the "communal concept" -- we often think in collective terms without sacrificing the importance of each individual without whom there can be no community.

Our parents were not brought up in pre-Christian homes. By conversion from African Traditional religion they accepted Christ early in their teens. They were baptized in the Methodist Church before they got married, making me a second generation Christian. Raising nine children -- three girls and six boys -- was not easy, but our parents were determined to send each of us to school -- mission schools. [In Zimbabwe parents have to pay fees in order to send their children to school from kindergarten on]. Not only did my parents set a good example for us; they also witnessed to their parents who later converted to Christianity, introduced in Zimbabwe by the American missionaries who came via Mozambique. Their life together was a living testimony of the goodness of God to their children, parents and the community at large.

For some years my parents lived in Chinyadza village in Tandi District. Our nearest town was Vengere, later named Rusape by the colonial rulers. Our homestead was composed of the main house and a separate hut, the kitchen. One could say our life revolved around the kitchen because this is where we cooked, ate, visited, prayed and fellowshipped. The main house was built with sun-baked bricks and had a lounge, parents' bedroom, boys' and girls' bedrooms.

In my view it is fair to classify my parents as responsible Christians who were dedicated to raising a Christian family. For example, they taught us certain articles of the Christian faith using *mwenje* to light up the room, (a kind of a glowing stick which served to provide light in the house at night). Thus we memorized the Lord's Prayer, the Apostles' Creed, the Catechism and various Bible verses. By example, they taught us to attend church every Sunday. Church was about nine miles (14.4 kilometres) away. I remember one of the favourite hymns sang at our local church at Chinyadza was: *"Tora zita rake Jesu, neurombo hwako hwese."* (Literally, take the name of Jesus, in spite of all your poverty).

Prayer was taken very seriously in our home by both parents but my mother was especially keen and focused. We were taught to pray when getting up in the morning and before going to bed in the evening. Breakfast, lunch and supper were all preceded by the appropriate thanks to the Lord. In addition to a life of prayer, our parents taught us to work hard. One could describe our parents almost as "workaholics". For example, they cleared 'a piece' of densely wooded land of about 100 acres using only a hoe and an axe. We had no choice but to work hard also.

Consequently, my family had plenty to eat and share with the less fortunate, or those who simply did not have enough. We had a well-balanced diet consisting of pork, chicken, and mutton that Dad raised. We also enjoyed game meat and fish which he caught whenever he went hunting or fishing in a nearby brook or in Nyagambu River when we lived in Old Mutare. But the staple food was vegetables with *sadza* made of maize or rapoko mealie meal. Occasionally we milked cows for home consumption only. Basically we lived off the land. Land was the main source of income was the land. My parents were among the leading peasant farmers, concentrating on raising maize, groundnuts and rapoko. At the end of the harvest season, we always had surplus to sell at the Grain Marketing Board.

Our father, Philemon Haadi, was one of the few individuals designated as pastor-teacher in the early times of the planting of the Church in Zimbabwe, at least in the Methodist Church which assigned him to schools like Ndingi, Old Mwandiambira and Mukahanana where he preached at the weekend and taught school during the week. As head of our family, he was a tough disciplinarian. He was a no nonsense kind of Christian who had read and fully understood the meaning of Proverbs 13:24. He was quite an inspirational weekday-teacher and weekend-preacher as well as a gifted musician, composer and vocalist.

Mother's favourite Scripture passage which seemed to preside over her life and upon which she based her task of guiding us daily in the Christian path was:

> *"Be devoted to one another in brotherly love. Honour one another above yourselves" (Rom.: 12:10") "Share with God's people who are in need. (13) " Live in harmony with one another. Do not be proud, but willing to associate with people of low position. Do not be conceited." (16) "Do not repay anyone evil for evil..."(17) " Do not take revenge my friend but leave room for God's wrath for it is written, It is mine to avenge: I will repay, says the Lord." (19)*

I am sure this is the reason all of her children and even grandchildren today are bound together with love, unity, peace and mutual respect. For example, the nine of us hold a family reunion in each sibling's home at least once a year. Mother believed in prayer like you and I know there is the sun and the moon. For her the power of prayer was as obvious and unquestionable as electric power.

She was truly a woman of prayer. I will return to my mother's amazing prayerfulness later in this book. Since Mom is late, my dear wife Maggie's prayerful life reminds me of our mother's life. As a dedicated Christian Maggie's prayers have sustained me in a wonderful way throughout my ministry! Back to mom: wherever we lived my mother was also renown for her hospitality to strangers. She was always prepared to invite passers-by to come in for a meal.

Our African culture influenced me through laws such as *usabe* (don't steal) *usauraye* (don't murder) etc. I belong to a culture that strongly teaches and expects us to respect all elders in the family and community. I must respect both the older brothers and sisters. In the community, I was expected to respect all men and women older than me. In return the extended family contributed to an abundant caring fellowship. I believe this is one more reason why, in Africa, if everything is equal, there are fewer people who get depressed or even lose their mind. In situations where someone loses their mind or material possessions, then family or relatives, even neighbours provide fellowship, food and shelter. The African culture has a network of caring people. Furthermore there are fewer old people's homes because the elderly normally move in with their children when they are too old to live by themselves. This is Jesus' love at work. Children take excellent care of their parents in their homes until death separates them. As Christians, we believe that at the point of death they have gone to be with God.

Born and raised during the colonial era, I have some ambivalence about colonialism. On the one hand there was a positive by-product namely the Gospel of Jesus Christ brought by missionaries who came on their own but later on collaborated with the colonialists. The missionaries evangelised our people through schools and hospitals. In fact, missionaries must be commended for not only bringing the Christian religion but secular education as well. Not only did they teach us to read but also they introduced new ways of taking care of ourselves -- personal hygiene. The large city populations made it necessary to observe certain public health rules. Ultimately, however, the onus was still with the African people who accepted the Bible, read it and interpreted it for themselves. Even in the early days of colonialism, I learned that the white foreigners known as 'the missionaries' were not as dangerous and as malicious as some extremists had wanted us to believe.

On the other hand, the missionaries actually collaborated with the colonialists who came expressly for the purpose of exploiting, conquering and ruling the natives. Colonialists came to rule by discrimination and oppression, as well as dehumanizing the indigenous people. Wherever mission schools were established, the founders committed themselves to teaching both religious and secular education. In a subtle way, this created a large reserve of barely literate, therefore useful, affordable and employable labour. So, clearly, colonialism was both fruitful and vicious at once. Old Mutare Mission Centre is the result of the former.[1]

---

[1] Chief Tendai of Manyika Land, recognizing that his people needed to learn skills, granted land and mining rights during the late 1800s to Cecil Rhodes in exchange for guns and educational opportunities.

I have vivid memories of how at Old Mutare Mission Centre, the oldest mission center of the United Methodist Church, the present home of Africa University, classes were cancelled during the Holy Week in order to concentrate on evangelic preaching from morning, afternoon through the evening. I will never forget one Holy Week meeting when Rev. Josiah Chimbadzwa preached. It was the morning service. Following the altar call, I felt/heard an inner voice (Jesus) saying: "Go to the altar." Simultaneously, I felt or heard another voice (Satan -- call it what you want) saying: "Don't go. You are too young . Your peers will laugh at you." (I was 13 years old.) The spiritual *Chimurenga* (warfare) in my soul went on for some minutes while other youth and adults were streaming toward the altar. And Jesus finally said: "Abel, this is the day of your Salvation. Go to the altar." I got up, went to the altar and knelt among others. My life was changed forever.

As part of the altar call management the pastor grouped us and assigned us to Samuel Munjoma[2], (then a theological student) who led our group to a nearby bush at the foot of Chiremba Mountain, that stands over the campus, for spiritual counselling. The purpose for this counselling was to make sure that I knew what was happening in terms of the decision I had just made. Also, if anyone had special needs, they would be addressed there. Convicted by the Holy Spirit I went straight to one of our missionaries who I believed I had wronged and confessed. Fortunately she graciously forgave me. I felt overwhelmed by a sense of having been born again from that day on.

II. ACCEPTING CHRIST PERSONALLY

Up until that day, although I was brought up in such a wonderful Christian home, I believe I had not personally met the Lord Jesus who was able to show

---

In 1898, Joseph Crane Hartzell, a Methodist bishop, stood on Chiremba Mountain above Old Mutare, Zimbabwe, (then called Old Umtali in rural Rhodesia), and looking down into the valley that is now home to Africa University envisioned hundreds of African young people with books in their hands, running to school.

Hartzell shared his dream with Rhodes and was granted a large tract of land at the base of Chiremba Mountain. This land was part of the original grant Rhodes received from Chief Tendai and had been, for a brief period, the settler town of Umtali. On that land, the United Methodist Church developed schools, an orphanage and a small hospital to serve the needs of the African people. ... ... (From: Africa University website.)

[2] By the way, this Rev. Samuel Munjoma found himself performing a major part in my spiritual life when he assisted the bishops who laid hands on my head when I was consecrated Bishop in Gaborone, Botswana, thirty two years later.

me unchristian attitudes and actions in my life. I dare say I was just a lukewarm Christian (nominal Christian) while in the house of the Lord. It is hard to believe yet there I was: born in a Christian home, taught all the Christian precepts, memorized the Lord's Prayer and all the creeds including the Apostles Creed, as I mentioned earlier, but I had not personally accepted Christ as my personal Saviour, until that day. One wonders how many people today are like that. They know of Jesus but *do not know* Him really.

There is a sense that I can say I was born twice, strangely, in the same general locale, Old Mutare. First, I was born on April 14, 1925 when my father was a student there. I was baptized as an infant by Rev. Horace Greeley, a missionary from the United States. The baptism ceremony took place in a little chapel, again at Old Mutare. The *second birth* occurred the same month of April, precisely 13 years later, in 1938 at the Easter Revival. By this time I was going to school.

Just as God had sent some faithful human beings to save me physically, since I was born prematurely, I believe God later sent His faithful ones, who, again contributed to my wholeness -- this time, spiritual salvation. This is especially striking considering that before the influence of Christianity in my country, Africans knew only one thing to do with premature babies: they put them in a clay pot, sealed it and buried it in cool ground, like near the river bank under certain trees, *mukute* or *mushakata*. But for the grace of God through the coming of Christian influences, this would have been my destiny. God saved me through Sister Beukerland, a missionary nurse from Sweden, who took the trouble to cover my whole body with cotton swathing.

Shortly after I was weaned from the special cotton swathing, I contracted a near fatal cough known as whooping cough -- a significant contributor to infant mortality at that time. My parents always reminded me that I narrowly escaped death during that sickness. A medicine man of Tsonzo, in Manicaland, Sekuru Joe Zinyembe, treated this disease in a matter of days, and I survived. Yes, a traditional healer saved my life. When I reflect on this incident, it causes me to re-evaluate the attitude of the church towards the African traditional healers, also referred to as herbalists or *n'anga*.

As if this was not enough, when I was two years of age, one day my mother was carrying me on her back, as all African mothers do. On this occasion a certain evil woman attempted to pass me food laced with poison -- right in church while my mother had her eyes shut in prayer along with other worshippers. By the grace of God, my aunt, Edith Mazire [nee Munangatire, mom's sister] who was in the back row, noticed the evil woman's fatal intent. She got up quickly and snatched the poisonous food before I ate it, got hold of the woman's arm and dragged her outside the sanctuary. Since the woman also had her own baby on her back, Auntie Edith commanded her to feed her own baby on the poisonous morsel. "Here is the food you were about to give my nephew," she declared. "If it is safe to eat then feed it to your own baby." Overcome with a sense of remorse, the woman started to sob. But that was not punitive enough. Auntie Edith concluded that her guess was correct, the food was indeed poisoned. So she started beating up this evil woman -- one punch sent the culprit to the ground! Here again, I was saved by God's grace -- Amazing Grace! Had Aunt Edith kept her eyes tightly shut with others, I would have accepted the lethal morsel.

I have only shared with you these three incidents where my life was threatened to substantiate the claim that God had a purpose for my life, and I feel I am under obligation to preach His love and everlasting goodness. There are many more threats and plots on my life that I survived especially when I was more actively involved in the liberation struggle for Zimbabwe. I know of five foiled attempts. Needless to say, I believe that I am alive by the grace of the Almighty God. At times I feel like John Wesley that I am a "pluck from the fire."

My parents also told me many things I did as a child between three and five years of age. Among them, they said I enjoyed playing church. For example they said I was quite fond of imitating the missionary preachers, especially Rev. Dr. M.J. Murphree. Each Sunday after church I would pluck leaves from *musekesa* or *mubhuku* tree, a Zimbabwean tree which has leaves that fold open like a book. Then I would tell my playmates to sit down and I would give them each a make-believe "hymnal" and I would "preach" to them. Playing church like this suggested to my parents that not only would I be a preacher, but an effective evangelist.

When I reflect upon the circumstances of my premature birth, sudden healing from the killer childhood disease -- whooping cough, escape from death by a witch, and the conversion at Old Mutare, abortive plots during my active political life, plus other dangers I did not even know about, I am thoroughly convinced that God created me to be one of His vessels to spread the Gospel to His people everywhere. Also, sometimes I feel like Paul who said: "Woe unto me if I don't preach the Gospel". And I believe that it is not by chance but by design that my first appointment after I graduated from the seminary was that of Assistant Director of Conference Evangelism in Zimbabwe in the United Methodist Church.

I feel strongly that though I hold a Theology Diploma, a Bachelor's degree in Religion and Philosophy, plus a Master's in Christian Education with emphasis on the Ministry to Youth, the most important credential is that God called me to preach the Gospel! That evangelism is the core of the Christian ministry has been my conviction throughout my service, whether in my capacity as bishop of the Zimbabwe Annual Conference, or as the Conference Youth Director. My ultimate credential for being an evangelist is *that calling* to "preach" the grace of God through Jesus Christ my saviour. Although I had refused the call for eight years, preferring to be a commercial farmer, I finally realized what God created me for.

Consequently, in writing this book on evangelism that decolonizes souls, I feel that my primary task is to bring people to Christ, even as Rev. Josiah Chimbadzwa introduced me to the Saviour. Furthermore, my Creator who called me to the holy ministry and anointed me, is the very One who saved me from various hazardous situations, and also spared me for this purpose. In addition to the fact that the Holy Spirit constantly re-fills me with His power, in writing this book, my burning desire is that Africa as well as the whole world be saved socially, politically, economically and of course, spiritually.

The flash of inspiration from Jesus said: "The harvest is ripe/plentiful, the labourers are few" (Luke 10:2). And I also heard the God of Ezekiel, who is also my God saying: "Son of man can these bones live?" (Ezek 37:3). Yes there is hope for accelerating of the rising up of Africa. Nothing is impossible with God. In fact in evangelism, *don't* and *impossible* are dirty words. I therefore invite and urge everybody to be one of the needed labourers of Jesus Christ. "Do the work of an evangelist" (II Timothy 4:5). The courage to do so comes from the fact that I too am a saved sinner -- a product of evangelistic preaching! I feel that now is our turn to evangelise the whole world, beginning with our respective local churches. My courage is fuelled with my awareness of how evil is rampant. I know the importance of repentance as the response to Christ's death on the cross. As St. Paul says, Christ died for us while we were yet sinners. Furthermore, I have experienced the meaning of "being filled" with the Holy Spirit. By the grace of God I have also experienced what it means to " bring someone to Christ". I know what difference all this can make in someone's life. More pressing is my belief that God wants us to bring others to Him so that He may receive them into life eternal.

Blessed are those who are used as God's vessels to bring others to salvation through Christ. Time will come when what Jesus assured us: "I am going there to prepare a place for you so that you may be where I am." (John 14:3) will materialize.

"May the grace of the Lord Jesus Christ, and the love of God, and the fellowship of the Holy Spirit be with you all" (2 Cor 13:14).

Two
THE GOSPEL IMPERATIVE

I. THE HARVEST IS RIPE (Luke 10:2)

When Jesus sent His disciples two by two to evangelise, He said: "The harvest truly is great, but the laborers are few; therefore pray the Lord of the harvest to send out laborers into His harvest" (NKJ Luke 10:2). This statement was true then, and in my opinion, is more so today. Numerous people in Zimbabwe and all over the continent are turning to Christ whenever the gospel is preached. Indeed, the harvest is ripe and great.

Before the seventy-two followers of Jesus returned to report the success story of their evangelism campaign to their commissioners, we can observe the Lord Jesus Himself had already predicted: "The harvest is so great but the labourers are few." Jesus also gives us an important hint. We are to pray to God so that He may send more workers. In this book, it is our belief that when God calls the evangelists, He equips them with the Holy Spirit who enables them to "seek" the lost.

The second observation is that the disciples reported their overwhelming success back to Jesus. "Lord, even the demons submitted to us in your name" (Luke 10: 17). To this Jesus' response was: "I saw Satan fall like lightening from heaven" (Luke 10: 18). One can read this to be Jesus' victory over the devil and the assurance that the war between Satan and God is won by those who evangelise in Jesus' name. Yes, Jesus' name has power to reclaim souls that are lost and those who are currently under the influence of the Devil.

One may ask; what are the sociological factors and the zeitgeist that moved Jesus to declare that *now* is the opportune time to call people into the Kingdom? Further, what ought to move us today?

By Jesus' estimation, the potential response to the harvest looked awesome -- great or plentiful. What lacked were more labourers to bring in the harvest. I think to embark on effective evangelism requires not only recognizing the need, having positive attitude and being enthusiastic about the outcome, but also actually going out there to invite people to God's salvation. This is why Jesus called Zacchaeus who was in need of salvation.

I believe, in principle no one can be an effective evangelist without a deep desire to see many people abandon their meaningless and sinful lives and turn to the Lord. Further, I am convinced that it is God's desire that people be saved (2 Pet. 3:9). This partnership is an important key to evangelism that decolonizes the soul, in partnership with Christ.

It was in the same spirit that I was moved to write this book. Both the conviction and the observation that African societies today are hungry and thirsty for righteousness (Matt. 5:6) compelled me to appeal to all who will read this book to heed the gospel imperative. In the case of Zimbabwe, throughout the country one sees gathering after gathering of people sitting under trees apparently listening to the gospel being preached. Furthermore, at any religious meetings across our nation, whether in sanctuaries, tents, class rooms, even on mountains, there is likely to be a potential convert because many are hungry and thirsty for the word of God. So many people -- hungry souls -- are searching for the meaning of life and trying to plumb the very depth, breadth, and height of their being. This is what Jesus observed in His Galilean days, and it is still true today, at least in Zimbabwe. If I may repeat, the harvest is great; it needs workers like you and me.

In the African context, (Zimbabwe in particular) one can effectively evangelise the masses who are turning from their old tribal, indigenous and homogeneous village existence to a pluralistic and heterogeneous urban and peri urban one, characterized by industrialized society. Yes, one can, because the gospel we preach cuts through ethnic and social boundaries. In fact, it is my conviction that Christ is the only real answer to the problems associated with the new industrial society emerging in Zimbabwe -- namely sin, immorality, corruption, stress induced mental illness, alcoholism, substance abuse, suicide, poverty, divorce, incest, etc. Nothing is needed more than preaching and practicing the Christian precepts in the new society. African people who used to belong to various tribal totems, now can share the "same" totem in Jesus Christ in the new society. Unity actually makes sense when our people know that humanity is all one family under the parenthood of God. To the fatherless, Christianity teaches God is our father -- father of all; to the have-nots, the gospel teaches that Christ came so they may have life and have it abundantly; to the friendless, a gospel hymn tells us: "What a friend we have in Jesus."

The human factor includes the enormous suffering of the masses on our continent due to gross misrule resulting from dictatorships and politically motivated massacres that are driving people into refugee camps and sending thousands into jail for merely holding a different political opinion. Starvation due to either failed crops or lack of skills or incompetent management of the economy has brought worse conditions to many nations on this continent. The HIV/AIDS pandemic has aggravated the situation. To all these situations, the message of Christian love brings the most needed answer. The Christian faith is a message of salvation to the whole person, i.e. both spiritually and physically. There are more factors than we have discussed here. Suffice it to say, people are devastated by ugly events and circumstances for which often they have no explanation or the ability to effectively control. In such a situation, we believe that Jesus Christ, the Lord of all Creation, will bring salvation to all flesh.

While both the hunger and the thirst for God and His righteousness are evident throughout the Third World, especially in Africa, at the same time the apparent apostasy in the West, demonstrated by the physical closures of sanctuaries because people have abandoned the church to worship the gods of materialism, is indicative of the need for the gospel which brings life's true meaning. Right now it seems that the beam of the Holy Spirit is tilting toward

Africa and we must respond " while Jehovah is still near" (Is. 55:6). Sadly we have to agree with Jack Nelson Pallmeyer who says in his book *Jesus Against Christianity*: " Malls are shrines where consumers go to worship and where they seek spiritual satisfaction." (Pallmeyer, 1980, 331). At these large shopping centres most Westerners are searching for contentment; unfortunately it is never to be found there because persons "...do not live on bread alone." (Matt. 4: 4). Nevertheless, that is the harvest waiting for us. On many occasions I have heard some of my American colleagues remark that we are in the era where African evangelists should preach the living Christ to the Americans! It is encouraging to realize that about 85% of the backsliders in the U.S.A know about Jesus. What they need is help to experience the risen Lord.

In Africa also, many are waiting for the invitation to experience the risen Lord. The suffering and the poverty of Africa, ironically, make it conducive to evangelising. Differently put, the conditions are favourable to raise a Christian giant of a church in Africa which will in turn preach the living Christ to Americans and elsewhere. Indeed the harvest is ripe!

The religio-political factor is also one reason why some 30 years ago I wrote *Rise Up and Walk*. This autobiography generally called for political liberation and subsequent establishment of Democracy. Now, I want to urge the African people to rise up and fly to the heights of holiness, righteousness, and freedom that Jesus the Christ can give to humanity. Let us preach the liberating gospel. If we don't, our hearts may turn as cold as those in the West who have to close their sanctuaries for the lack of active membership. And I want to warn that Africa without Jesus can be like a beautiful house fully furnished but without light. Jesus is the light of the world. His presence is not compatible with greed, corruption, self-centeredness and oppression, which cause most of our people to suffer.

The harvest is truly ripe and Jesus is commanding: "As the father has sent me, I am sending you" (John 20:21). So Christian youth, men, women, and both the laity and clergy, there is the challenge! May the grace, peace, power of the Holy Spirit of Pentecost be with you always! Amen.

II. GOD'S LOVE (John 3:16)

"Dear friends, let us love one another. For love comes from God. Every one who loves has been born of God and knows God. Whoever does not love, does not know God because God is love" (I John 4:7-8). Clearly, John makes the point that our knowledge of God is expressed through our love for each other. This is one compelling reason why we must evangelise in Africa. The love of God in our lives equips us to love others. If we love our fellow human beings we are compelled to commit ourselves to their welfare, their health and wholeness in general. In the same chapter, John also draws the conclusion that one cannot claim to love God if one does not love physical beings one can actually see. Love is not just an abstract thing -- it is real, tangible and of God.

The best and most godly thing we can do for others on this planet is lead them to Christ. The Saviour leads the convert from death to life, from darkness to light, from confusion to focused life. We agree with Scott T. Jones that "To evangelise non-Christian persons without loving them fully is not to evangelise. To love non-Christian persons without evangelising them is not to love them well" (Jones, 2003, 21).

.God's love is also inclusive. John 3:16 tells us "God so loved the world that He gave His one and only son that whoever believes in Him shall not perish but have eternal life." God loves the world including Africa, which badly needs a lot of loving. She has ugly scars of colonialism and suffers from unhealed deep wounds of neo-colonialism, pseudo democracies and outright oppressive sovereign governments. Africa also suffers from coup after coup and wars caused by lack of Christian love for each other, a depraved sense of what constitutes human dignity, and misunderstanding of what Christian stewardship entails. People live as refugees in camps and as victims in their own continent. Sad! It makes my heart bleed. The fact that people still have to live in Diaspora is a loud cry that Africa needs a lot of loving. The masses are obviously hungry and thirsty for true freedom and the abundant life Christ promises every one. Africa cries a lot from the pain of starvation, famine and that ugly and deadly monster called "poverty", which not only constitutes a hell on earth for the living but sends millions to their graves. If unborn children had a choice, some would decide *not* to be born in Africa because of the conditions stated above. It is not an exaggeration to say dogs and cats live more comfortable lives in most developed countries than most children do in Africa. The love of God through genuine Christians would make a big difference if all Christians observed 1 John 4:7 cited above.

Those who contribute to the misery, poverty and suffering of the children by causing wars, spreading disease, perpetuating ignorance and fostering laziness must be converted and they must let the children live an abundant life which Christ came to deliver to everyone. God who created us in His own image also commands: "love your neighbour as yourself." (Matt. 22:39). Apparently, if we love God as ourselves, then there is no real reason why we should not love our neighbour who, like us, was created in God's image. God's love has the power to make us of one accord -- with the power to forgive, to provide, to be gracious and to be called the children of God. By presenting the whole gospel for the whole person, we shall have loved our dear brother and sister with God's love. Anything less than a whole gospel is equivalent to offering partial or conditional love -- which is not God's love.

In a country like Zimbabwe, where the present ruling party treats members of the opposition as "enemies" of the state, genuine Christians are strongly urged to obey and live by Jesus' commandment to love their neighbour as themselves. Although there over 2000 different Languages and dialects spoken in Africa, the gospel is being communicated. The love and the peace of God that passes all understanding can create the avenue of love, unity, peace and liberty. This is what Africa needs badly if it should be *an imitation of heaven on earth.* Our country could be characterized with love, peace, unity, freedom, security, wholeness and prosperity. This is not too idealistic, rather it is the challenge that Jesus gives to Christians when He says "you are the salt of the earth" (Matt. 5:13) and "you are the light of the world" (Matt. 5:14).

How I wish the principle of *the imitation of heaven on earth* would take root in every country in Africa. If I had to put my name to a tenet, this would be the one, for this is how God intended it to be. Simply stated, life on earth should be a mirror image of heaven. One clear sign that this has been achieved is when a lot of people who left their respective countries want to and will come back to the mother continent -- Africa. This expectation can only be fulfilled by praying to God that He may anoint rulers who love and fear Him, rulers who truly and earnestly desire to create genuine democracies for their respective countries. Hynm 324 "Mwari Tumanyi Vasandi" in *Ngoma dze*United Methodist Church yeZimbabwe is on this theme.

Africans of all shades and religious faiths need to view themselves as children of one parent, belonging to one continent, under one creator -- God. Traditionally this God is called by many different names (as we will discuss in Chapter Three) but is one and the same loving God. It is this God who "so loved the world that He gave His only begotten son…" (John 3:16).

It never ceases to amaze me how and why Africans fight among themselves in spite of our general poverty and homogeneity. We sometimes behave like irrational creatures. Let me share an incident I witnessed at my rural cottage. One time our turkey hatched six chicks. We put the chicks in a nice warm cage in our kitchen. They received superb love and care. About the same time, I bought two eight-week old pigs to rear. They too got special care, though outside the house. I provided them with everything they required in order to grow.

I must admit that I was very disappointed and upset to observe that the six beautiful turkeys were often fighting each other. The same was true with the pigs until one of the pigs was actually killed in a fight. The incident got me thinking: Why fight? Is God making a point to me from this "parable?" When I theologized this incident, I concluded this is how God must be disturbed about His highest creation, *humans* who live by quarrelling, hatred, fighting even murdering each other. God must be disappointed when we live like animals without a sense of peace, love, respect for life and the like. When God created the universe and human kind in His image, the Bible says "... everything was very good."(Gen. 1:18) So where does evil come from among us?

It seems to me as long as we believe that God is a moral Being, then He must be hurt, saddened and even shocked by human's dislike, misunderstanding and outright hatred of each other. This happens between husbands and wives, parents and children, neighbours, village communities, church members and nations. Why do we not let God's love rule in our lives and the world? With James, we must ask: "What causes fights and quarrels among you? Don't they come from your desires that battle within you?" (James 4:1). I think our only hope for peace among human beings is if every heart receives Christ, the Prince of Peace, whom God has graciously given to all creation. Our prayer must be that Africa is filled with music of the love of God.

III. THE NEED FOR SALVATION/WHOLENESS (JOHN 3:3)

Jesus said to the notorious, hated and sinful tax collector, "Zacchaeus come down immediately. I must stay at your house today" (Luke 19:5). Those who are in partnership with Christ through the Holy Spirit today still heed this invitation to salvation since there are more sinners now than when Jesus walked in Galilee.

The reason we should evangelise in Africa is because there is need for salvation, wholeness. Defined theologically, salvation is generally understood as "deliverance from sin and penalties of sin, redemption." Salvation is sometimes interpreted to refer solely to the Judgement Day. However, in this book the concept is used to designate both physical and spiritual wholeness -- immediately. In this discussion on salvation we will confine ourselves to salvation from (1) the Devil (Satan) (2) and sin.

The Devil

Whether one prefers the term Devil or Satan, the referent is the same. In philosophy of religion, scholars tend to dwell on the philosophical question of " existence." Such is not our intent here. I think there is such a thing as the Devil or a Satan-spirit that causes people to do evil things or entertain evil thoughts. Here we shall call the spirit that often tempts us to sin, "Satan" (Luke 10:18). Peter called it " the devil" (1 Pet. 5:8). Like Jesus, Paul named it "Satan" (2 Corinthians. 12:7). Therefore as long as there is no theologian or scientist who has disproved the influence of this wicked tempting spirit, we will continue to believe it exists. (Science cannot prove things spiritual anyway). All we know is that spiritual giants have wrestled with this force known as Satan. Jesus battled with it "... the devil...," "... Satan...'(Matt. 4:1-10). The human race has from time immemorial been harassed, terrorized and destroyed by evil. It must have its master, at least it has some influence on events or to produce evil, pain, failure, or some such adversity.

Chief enemy of the human race: Sin

Sin is generally defined as "the wilful breaking of religious or moral law." In this discussion we choose to confine ourselves to the Christian faith. What is sin? To illustrate what sin is, let me share this particular incident.

When I was in primary school at Hartzell, one of my classmates, Alec Chapata became ill. He was from Maramba Pfungwe, the north-eastern district of Zimbabwe. His entire body was infested with boils. Fortunately there was a very reputable physician practising at Penhalonga, a few miles from Old Mutare, Doctor Montgomery. So Alec went to see this physician who gave him a rather unusual prescription. " I want you to buy 30 oranges and go back to the dorm. Eat only one orange per day until they are finished," said the doctor. Alec was terribly disappointed with the good doctor and had the nerve to challenge the doctor's practice. " I thought you were going to give me an injection, or prescribe some kind of medicine." The doctor firmly repeated his instruction with an assurance that he was going to be fine if only he would follow the instruction. Because the doctor was firm, Alec succumbed. Sheepishly he went and did what the doctor told him.

At the end of 30 days plus, Alec's boils had disappeared. His body healed nicely. What had happened? Obviously, Alec's blood was hungry and thirsty for vitamin C, which is found in oranges. So the boils where a warning sign of that fact. The absence of vitamin C in Alec's body caused gross discomfort and pain. This incident is analogous to sin.

What is sin? When our souls are not in contact with the real spiritual vitamin C -- Christ, we break down. We suffer and may even die. When we refuse to accept the Saviour, when we dishonour our Maker, when we are disobedient to God's law, we are in sin. That status will eventually destroy us.

I believe that when the church spends lots of money, energy and time telling people "don't use drugs, don't drink, don't smoke, don't engage in perverted sexual lifestyles, is only dealing with indicators or symptoms (like boils on Alec's body) but the real cause must ultimately be addressed -- they must be filled with Jesus Christ in their lives, the vitamin C of the soul.

George E. Morris put it this way " when people refuse to allow God to be the centre of their lives, then selfishness with its isolation, emptiness and loneliness becomes their lot. They refuse God and theirs becomes a life without purpose, meaning or hope. They let their lower self have its own way and eventually they discover that there is nothing left but death" (Morris, 1986, 85). Relative to sin, Paul would say: "For the wages of sin is death, but the gift of God is eternal life in Christ Jesus our Lord." (Rom. 6:23).

IV. SALVATION IS AVAILABLE

Africa does not need to live under the power and yoke of sin and the devil, when the church of Jesus Christ is on the continent. The gospel is now available almost in every major language or dialect, as we have already pointed out.

For over 80 years I have lived on this planet on both sides of the Atlantic ocean; I have seen many people who are slaves to sin; I have also known individuals, groups, and families, who have been saved through Jesus Christ. To Joseph and Mary the Angel said you will "...give birth to a son, ... He will save His people from their sins" (Matt. 1:21). This is printed in every Bible which most African people are now able to read for themselves, "for the Son of Man came to seek and save what was lost" (Luke 19:10). Since the Scriptures are now used everywhere on the continent, this is the time to broadcast the seed of faith so that those willing may pick it up and grow and live.

Repentance

We have stated elsewhere in this book that John the Baptist, Jesus Christ,

Peter, Paul, some prophets and the New Testament gospel all advocate repentance unto salvation. Likewise today, people must proclaim the gospel that decolonizes the soul. Every spirit-filled preacher must beat the devil and sin out of God's people so they may be saved. Spirit-filled preaching is one of the ways we usher people to Christ. In turn He touches them with His grace unto repentance. And what is true repentance? "To feel sorry for an error, ...to feel such regret over a wrong action, ...to change one's mind," is repentance. Apostle Paul says " Godly sorrow brings repentance that leads to salvation and leaves no regret...." (2 Corinthians 7:10). This is repentance.

When we witness Christ to others and lead them to a point where they feel genuine sorrow for their wrong doing to fellow human beings or to God, we are evangelising. When they turn away from their sinful life, that is repentance. Genuine sorrow and repentance takes place when a person is convicted with the Holy Spirit. So evangelism is guiding persons towards genuine repentance.

I agree with Morris that "repentance comes as a response to the good news that God has taken the initiative on our behalf..." (Morris, 1980, 123). Thus, repentance and subsequent forgiveness of sin, is a major aspect of salvation or wholeness. Christ is the author of such wholeness, and He has already paid the price for this now free gift of eternal life.

Conversion

Conversion, like birth, is a necessary process of one's spiritual journey. *Spiritual rebirth or new birth* is the beginning of one's eternal journey. Jesus said "I tell you the truth, no one can see the Kingdom of God unless he is born again." (John 3:3). When Jesus said these words, He was talking to Nicodemus, a Jew, a polished Pharisee, one of the very top leaders of the Jews who did not miss Sabbath. Nicodemus was not some homeless man. He fasted twice per week, tithed on everything that came his way and kept the law from childhood. He was an educated and good member of his "church." This man believed in and worshipped one God, the creator of the world. Yet he did not understand this simple statement.

Indeed, this apparently simple yet mind boggling statement sparked a major doctrinal discussion which is still controversial to this day. Maybe the statement was not that simple after all. Furthermore, this is a truth that Pharisees sought to understand in studying the Torah. Here is the simple Jesus who says to him: "I tell you the truth, no one can see the kingdom of God unless he is born again." (John 3:3).

From this passage therefore, we have the gospel teaching about the second birth. Further we remind ourselves that this doctrine did not originate with Paul or the Pope or Martin Luther or John Wesley or John Calvin or Karl Barth or Billy Graham or any of the great Christian leaders we know. Rather, it was taught by Jesus Christ Himself. Therefore conversion is a crucial step which one must undergo in order to be a transformed person. Only when a person is born anew can one become a citizen of the Kingdom of God. I believe that there is nothing conservative or liberal about this.

Jesus was against externalism and He battled the Pharisees about this. He was trying to show His audience that true salvation comes through rebirth. True conversion transpires when one has been born again -- washed with water yes but born of the spirit, that is. Since Jesus Himself taught the necessity for the second birth -- *rebirth*, why is it that there is a lot of controversy surrounding the doctrine of "being born again?"

Perhaps this is one of the reasons why based on George Barna's research, it was discovered that quite a lot of people in the church today, do not have any personal relationship with Christ, in spite of being in church for a long, long time. They have not experienced *spiritual rebirth*. They are present day Nicodemuses. Like him, they are not necessarily bad people -- they just have not experienced *spiritual rebirth*.

There is quite an alarming number out there who are clueless about rebirth, personal knowledge of Jesus, in-filling by the Holy Spirit, and consequently cannot teach or preach about rebirth. The kind of church they form is bound to be spiritually weak, cold, sick and slowly dying. Many main line denominations are experiencing this slow death because they have conveniently ignored preaching rebirth. I believe that a church that has not and does not believe in spiritual rebirth "cannot see the kingdom of God," as Jesus said. In fact, now we can reverse Nicodemus' question to say: " How can a congregation be a church unless it has experienced rebirth?"

True salvation will come from preaching the total gospel for the whole person leading to total conversion or second birth, i.e. spiritual birth. My prayer is that Africa and the whole world starts now to take Jesus more seriously. Those called to evangelise must preach the Jesus who declared that the correct way to see the Kingdom of God is by being born again, not just by water but by the spirit of Jesus the Christ.

In closing this section let me briefly deal with two questions.

Is conversion possible without genuine repentance? ... No!

Is conversion possible without evangelism? ... Yes!

V. TRANSFORMATION OF THE HUMAN CONDITION (Luke 19:10)

In sociological, political, and theological terms, the human condition is generally characterized by chronic brokenness. For instance, consciously or unconsciously, some people believe that their existence or survival depends on the demise or non-existence of any other human being that does not belong to their group or kind. Hence, these people live on the presumption that in order to thrive, everyone else must suffer; in order to climb the social ladder everyone else must be down trodden; therefore it is justified for others to starve while they have food to throw away. This is why the world has people who can only view their tomorrows in relation to beating out of existence other peoples' companies, races, families etc. Worse still, the human condition very often deteriorates into less than human state of affairs which Dr. Mwalimu Julius Nyerere, former

President of Tanzania characterized as a "Man eat dog" situation. I call it the decadence of the spirit.

The human condition is often characterized by misery and tragically by wretchedness whenever persons choose to live outside God's law. Just as Artistotle once said Man (sic) (Human) perfected by society is the best of all animals. He (sic) is the most terrible of all when he (sic) lives without the law and without justice.

Furthermore, worst of all, the human condition is characterized by injustice and a gross lack of human compassion. Lacking both justice and practical compassion, humankind can only be transformed by preaching and hearing the Gospel of Jesus the Christ who is the very channel and embodiment of God's justice and compassion. The Bible declares that Jesus is the Light of all nations -- the saviour of the human race. Samuel Johnson (1709 - 1784) an English author also once declared; "Christianity is the highest perfection of humanity." Based on what God, the creator of humanity, intended for the human race, it must be that only this faith can perfect the human condition.

Wrestling with the struggle to perfect the human condition, Paul says

> "but I see another law at work in the members of my body, waging war against the law of my mind and making me a prisoner of the law of sin at work within my members. What a wretched man I am! Who will rescue me from this body of death? Thanks be to God through Jesus Christ our Lord! So then, I myself in my mind am a slave to God's law, but in the sinful nature a slave to the law of sin"(Rom 7:23-25).

And he writes to the church at Rome: "if you confess with your mouth that Jesus is Lord and believe in your heart that God raised Him from the dead, you will be saved" (Rom 10:9). What Paul does here is to externalize salvation. Unlike some eastern religions that believe that "you are your own saviour", Christianity believes that *Jesus is*. So we must preach the name of Jesus by which we are saved.

Thus the human condition compels us to evangelise humanity by every means possible and with every ounce of energy that God put in all those who hear and obey the gospel imperative. In fact, to obey this imperative is a major step toward the execution of God's plan for our redemption. The human condition of chronic *lostness* compelled Jesus to associate with not only the poor but also the sinners, whoever they were. It is important and never to be forgotten that Jesus clearly stated His purpose or mission, when He said: "For the son of man came to seek and save…" (Luke 19:10).

The salvation promised here does not only end with the individuals, the family, the nation, but must include the whole human race because such is God's will "that all creation may see its salvation." In His divine foreknowledge, God has made a provision for humanity's salvation in Jesus the Christ. Through Him we believe the transformation of ethnic groups, the culture, customs, politics, government, economy and indeed the entire human condition on the continent of

Africa will be affected.

VI. THE LIBERATION OF THE OPPRESSED (Luke 4:18-19)

Jesus' statement that those who are well have no need for a physician was deep insight for all time. Similarly, there is an African proverb that says: *"Mwana asingachemi anofira mumbereko,"* -- meaning if one who is suffering does not speak up, he or she may actually die in that state. Jesus knew such deep human yearnings because the Spirit of God was upon Him. No doubt, Jesus chose this passage: The spirit of the Lord is upon me, because He has anointed me to preach good news to the poor. He has sent me to proclaim freedom for the prisoners and recovery of sight for the blind, to release the oppressed, to proclaim the year of the Lord's favour" (Luke 4:18-19). It does not take a rocket scientist to understand that Jesus was aware of His saviour role and was prepared to carry out that function at all cost.

The very concept " Liberation" tends to trigger a certain response or reaction in the oppressed as well as in the oppressors. Luke 4:18-19 sends hope that Jesus may bring liberation. As Paul puts it, we can be a new creation, liberated from the old shackles and chains of a life that is governed by the devil. So I believe that Jesus brings liberation through His gospel. And, therefore, properly presented, the gospel of Jesus Christ has the power to set at liberty the oppressed. If done the *right way* -- the Christ way, both the oppressed and the oppressors will experience liberation in Jesus Christ because in Him there is neither Jew nor Greek, slave nor freed, male nor female, for you are all in Christ Jesus (Gal 3:28). So, true and full liberation must start with personal spiritual liberation, which promotes holiness in one's life. But holiness is limited if it is imprisoned by surrounding forces that dehumanize a person. One may be politically, socially or intellectually free, but spiritually a detainee of sin. To this state of affairs, Jesus says: "what does it benefit a person to gain the whole world but lose one's soul?" (Matt. 16:26)

This leads us to say that one of the reasons we must evangelise in Africa is because the entire continent needs liberation badly and urgently. Africa needs to be set free. In saying this I refer to the type of liberation that is given in the name and the spirit of Jesus who declared " I have come that they may have life, and have it to the full" (John 10:10). That is the kind of life every normal human being needs to have and expects. Where is this abundant life? one may rightfully ask. With all the mushrooming Christianity in Africa, where is this life? Do we have it?

While Africa is blessed with plenty of sunshine, a culture that is hospitable, a loving and caring extended family system that drastically reduces loneliness and provides a caring environment until one dies, there is still a ghost of oppression left by colonialism and neo-colonial mentality. I firmly believe that what we need in Africa today is the "Son who sets us free indeed." (John 8:36). Ironically, when we are set free to be who God created and intended for us to be, then and only then can we be meaningfully productive. For example, when Zacchaeus received salvation he gave more to the community than he ever did when he lived in sin. The sin of greed on the continent has contributed to the suffering of the masses. The question one may ask is, "How long, Oh Lord?" The answer is sad: until we all perish.

The Politics of Oppression

Can Africa be truly free? Today numerous Africans are still politically oppressed in a number of countries. With the exception of South Africa, which has created a constitution that is second to none, many nations lack a true sense of freedom because their governments do not understand the concept of loyal opposition, for example. Allow me to share how I personally experienced oppression at the hands of my own national government.

In Zimbabwe, after Mr. Robert G. Mugabe was declared "winner" of the 1980 election, I did what I believe was a rare thing in the Africa of that time. I went to his office to congratulate him on his "victory". Since he was my successor, I felt it fair to wish him well in that office. I told him that I would support him when he was right; I would also oppose him whenever he did things that were not conducive to freedom, democracy and prosperity for Zimbabwe. I knew that if Black people were to rule our own country properly -- with focused determination -- we had to work on reconciliation; and that was a pledge on my part to mount loyal opposition. In response, I was detained in jail for ten months without trial. He alleged that I had three secret armies in South Africa, Israel and Zaire (now Democratic Republic of Congo) that were all ready to overthrow the government. This is why I had gone to Israel.

Of course that was all false. The truth is every bishop in the United Methodist Church, the world over, is entitled to three months of study leave every four years. I chose to go to Israel to study at the Jerusalem Centre of Biblical Studies for six weeks. I spent four weeks touring places that mark the events as they are recorded in the Bible. Then I returned home. But only three days after I returned, oppressors seized me. Ten months later, I was released because all allegations were false. One could not help but link such treatment at the hands of one's own people to the Calvary event.

Based on Jesus' teaching to "forgive those who sin against you," I have long forgiven them.

This is only one example of how some African governments treat their opposition parties. To be an opposition party in some countries in Africa is to be declared "an enemy of the government." Opposition members live in fear for their lives. Their opposition voice is regarded as a declaration of war against the ruling party, which is viewed as synonymous with government. Some governments are even worse than the colonial past. For example, in Zimbabwe's colonial period, whites knew Africans had a different party, yet there was not as much intimidation and killing as we experience today.

There is however the hope that there will be freedom, liberty and democracy in Africa. I know it because a few years ago before I retired from active politics,

I asked a bright young lawyer to conduct a comparative study of constitutions of the world. Maybe we could be inspired to write a new constitution for Zimbabwe. He studied 33 constitutions and reported to me that "…there is none that surpasses the constitution of South Africa: not even that of the United States." South Africa has a constitution conducive to liberty, freedom and democracy. I was happily surprised, and highly encouraged because I believe in democracy. I love democracy. I dream, hope, and pray for a democratic Africa. There is hope in southern Africa because one of our big countries, South Africa, has a constitution that guides their government to true democracy. Thank God for creating His child Nelson Mandela, the first President of a free South Africa. I am convinced South Africa is off to a good start; the recent events in their presidium vindicates my position, but the leadership has to always be faithful to the spirit of that governing document.

It will be a great, new, bright and happy day when Africa will put in place respective democracies for her nations. Some of us will keep praying and hoping, for Africa's leaders to mature enough to stop in-group fighting, economic corruption, general negligence and violence. My prayer is for African nations to see the day when Africans can carry passports continentally, without requiring expensive visas; when we have one type of currency, opposition political parties can have their voice and play their role of loyal opposition without being treated as though they were enemies of the ruling party. It seems interesting that what I am praying for (in our future), is already happening in parts of the European Union (as well as being challenged). We desire to see the day when after persons have been spiritually born again, they can live freely in their native land.

I know that when Christians talk about liberty and freedom from the pulpit, the common reaction or response we get from the world politicians is, "Stay out of politics. You have no business in politics." Of course that is not true. It is just ignorance on the part of such politicians.

As citizens, taxpayers and voters, we are entitled to a political opinion. The true gospel of Jesus is for the whole person. As long as one is a religious, social, physical, psychological and spiritual being, one must be totally liberated. In fact, the church needs to be deeply involved especially when the brand of politics being practiced dehumanizes God's children. We need to tell the politicians, in love and charity, that while there is no place for secular politics in Christianity, there is a definite place for Christianity in politics.

Jesus commands us to go into the *world* and be the "salt" or the "light" of the earth. This means Christians are expected to take a leading role in the governance affairs of their nations. Politics is one of those worlds. I agree with the thinking that when politicians tell the church to "Stay out of politics," they are meddling in Jesus' liberating business. When they oppress God's children or misrule them, they are breaking the law of God which is greater than any law passed by any worldly ruler. As Jesus' messengers it is our Holy responsibility to insist on morality in politics and the government by our voice and influence. It is our business to salt the earth and light the world.

In concluding this section, we pose this question: why do politicians cry foul at clergy but not at accountants, doctors, journalists or even lawyers? Why clergy, and why especially Christian clergy? Could it be they are validating the need for Christians in politics? Of course, it is preferred that politicians themselves be Christians, or at least God-fearers governed in their own lives with Christian principles from deep in their hearts. However, for as long as they continue in their *lostness,* it is the role of Christians to illuminate secular politics for the sake of better governance, in keeping with God's will for His people.

Liberation from Poverty

The deadly order of the day in Africa is poverty. Today people die from lack of food, medicines and medical attention because they can't afford or access them when they need it. For example as I write this book, in Zimbabwe we need a doctor for every 16,000 people. Most general practitioners and specialists have been swept away by the brain drain to better managed and free countries. The wealth is still in the hands of those who made it from exploiting slave labour and those who have amassed it by stealing from public funds taking advantage of impunity they enjoy from privilege. Land reform is one big step toward reduction of poverty if it is done peacefully, transparently, strategically and systematically. Liberation from poverty to prosperity is what it says, to "have life and have it abundantly," as Jesus said (John 10:10).

Women's Liberation

Experience has taught us that the Christian church, through the arm of education, preaching and teaching in Jesus' name has freed millions of Africans from ignorance, witchcraft, fear, and superstition. But there are still more oppressive structures in our culture. Thus the burden must be on us to continue to be the light of the world. For instance, the oppression of women still goes unchecked. Of course, in saying this I do not purport to be their liberator because I know they will free themselves. Sexism is an evil.

A few months ago when I visited Rusape, the town nearest my rural cottage, I saw a woman about 4 foot 8 inches tall (1.4 meters), carrying her baby on her back while pushing a cart full of goods. In Zimbabwe it is not unusual to see her pushing the cart with one hand while the other hand helps her balance a big load on her head plus a one or two year old child trailing her. When I see such scenes, it reminds me once more that something still needs to be done about the issue of women's lives in Africa. In discussing evangelism on the continent, I would be remiss if women's liberation was not included.

Generally speaking the liberation of women is an important matter especially in countries that are fairly liberated. One may take Kwame Nkrumah's adage one notch higher, by saying unless all oppression is eliminated on the continent, we are still not free. To start with, man has been characterized by a despising attitude toward women. Kwame remarked that Ghana's freedom is not meaningful until all African colonies were free. (Ghana was the first colony to gain independence in 1958). Some men subscribe to this but suddenly suffer from "double standards" when it comes to liberation of women. Advocating the liberation of women from oppression by men can be traced back to the Bible where we see Jesus working with women like Mary Magdalene. He once said: "…Go instead to my brothers and tell them I am returning to my father and your father, to my God and your God" (John 20:17) From this site, Mary became the first to proclaim, " I have seen the Lord!" (John 20:18). Jesus' own mother was the carrier of God in her womb! What an honour!

Because Jesus saw it fit to announce His resurrection sermon through Mary, women deserve all honours in the Christian religion. Furthermore, women support the Church in greater numbers than men. If therefore God chooses to work with women as well as men, neither one should claim an upper hand in the Church. Certainly, women should be allowed to preach because God calls preachers and prophets. If Jesus chose a woman to preach the first resurrection sermon, who are we to say women must not preach. Although Paul encouraged us to give a lower seat to women in the church (perhaps for cultural correctness of his time), that is not Jesus' example. The Master's example was to treat all human beings as equals -- both women and children whom men generally relegate to the periphery.

One of the reasons for evangelising in Africa is that women become free from all forms of oppression. Women experience political oppression together with men in many nations. In addition, they get gender oppression with regards to employment. Although the tendency is now being eliminated, for the longest time women were paid less than men for the same type of job, even though they have the same academic training, and same hierarchical needs.

Look at a woman out there in the village. She gets up together with her husband to span their oxen to plough. They plough until lunchtime (about 11:00 a.m.). The husband sits down resting while the wife continues to work-preparing lunch for the family. After lunch they go back to the field to work again. Then about 5:00 p.m. they unyoke their oxen for the evening. Again, the husband gets to relax and rest while the wife prepares supper. The woman rests only when she goes to bed. But if there is a church section meeting, she may have to attend that too!

Christian individuals and the church need to be quite intentional about our attitudes toward women: our relationships, customs, culture and behaviour as it relates to women. We need to examine and frequently re-examine our attitudes to see if they are in harmony with Christian principles today. Women, like men, deserve to be free -- totally free -- to be responsible through the power of the Holy Spirit. In our dealings with women, we need to be guided by Jesus' teaching when He said, "…so in everything, do to others what you would have them do to you, for this sums up the Law and the Prophets' (Matt. 7:12).

At the end of Chapter Three we discuss aspects of culture that are inconsistent with Christian principles. The African male must re-examine this issue. We need to be intentional about dismantling any oppressive systems, whether cultural or doctrinal. Since women are a significant percentage of the population they must be challenged to rid themselves of the oppressive yoke.

Men also must be intentional about joining hands with women in the struggle to get rid of all practices that dehumanize women. Unfortunately, society is always too slow to change. However there seems to be a ray of hope, a thread of evidence that women are now standing shoulder to shoulder with men in education, medical work, government, offices in church, and in business. And we know a lot of that has come through Jesus Christ. The church of Jesus Christ must continue to work hard to effect women's liberation.

To women, I say, be of good courage! Remember Paul said to Timothy: "Don't let any one look down on you because you are young, but set an example for the believers in speech, in life, in love, in faith and in purity" (1 Timothy 4:12). Likewise, I say to all my sisters in the faith, don't let anyone look down on you because you are women, but assert yourselves, as children of God, created in the image of God. Work out your liberation, and may God's grace be with you!

VII. HUMANITY'S YEARNING FOR ETERNITY

Various cultures and religions have developed theories and even theologies that seek to explain humanity's yearning for eternal life. F.W. Robertson (1816-1853) argued: " Every natural longing has its satisfaction. For instance, if we thirst, God has created liquids to gratify thirst; if we are susceptible of attachment, there are beings to gratify love; if we are thirsty for eternal life then it is likely that there is an eternal life and eternal love to satisfy that craving." Of course, there is also yearning that originates from vanity. But what we have here is a concern for this worldwide yearning for eternal life.

To begin this discussion on the topic of eternal life, the most logical source to turn to is the Bible, which discusses the beginning, existence and end of everything that was created, including the human being. If "eternal" means no beginning, no ending, "we can only find its meaning in God whose beginning and ending is without limits. Thus, when we partner with Christ we may begin to feel a sense of the meaning of " eternity." Paul puts it in his famous discourse on love in his letter to the Corinthians: "Love never ends" (1 Cor. 13:8). St. Augustine of Hippo is also well known for his soul touching and moving testimony in his confessions: *"Our hearts are restless until they find the rest in thee, O God."* Hence the necessity to evangelise people. Humanity has this unquenchable yearning for eternity.

As previously stated, those who seek life's meaning do well to seek God the author of life. That which drives them to seek life's meaning is in fact a yearning for eternity; only God can provide that -- most adequately and completely. Only He can satisfy the hunger that they feel deep within themselves. It is for this reason that the Bible cites one lawyer asking: "What must I do to inherit eternal life?" (Luke 10:25) because He is the source and guarantor of eternal life. Therefore, every serious believer is obligated to proclaim the good news of Jesus Christ, the author of eternal life. He is the only one who most adequately satisfies the human yearning (hunger and thirst) for eternal life. At the end of

Luke's gospel, the risen Lord commanded that the ultimate goal or purpose of His resurrection is that "the message of repentance.... for the forgiveness of sins must be preached to all the nations with all the authority given to the believers by the risen Lord of Life. So unless believers evangelise, then those who are hungry and thirsty for eternal life will remain unsatisfied. They can not get satisfaction from just reading the Scriptures. One must believe that Jesus is the saviour, the Son of God.

One more point of clarification must be made here. Eternal life does not start after death, as many tend to think. I believe those who live in Christ are already in the midst of eternal living. *It starts now.* Think about this. It is quite exciting to comprehend it. When a person has accepted Jesus Christ, forsaken his/her sin and started living with and for Him, following Him and obeying Him, that person has already entered the "eternal orbit." When death comes, one just throws off the jacket [*chihovorosi*] called body and continues to live in eternal life.

You see, Jesus did not say to the rich young ruler; "You must drop dead now so you go into eternal life." No. He said, "Do this and you will live" (Luke 10:28). Eternal life is action-filled living, not death. When the rich young ruler asked Jesus, " What shall I do to inherit eternal life? (Luke 18:18), he should have actually asked; what must I do to live an active life with you, the author of life? Jesus' answer was essentially: "Spread yourself amongst the poor of the earth, giving significance and meaning to their lives and find your significance in their lives." Living with Christ who dwells among the least of these is the essence of eternal life.

Another man -- a rich young man also asked Jesus; "Good teacher, what must I do to inherit eternal life?" (Luke 18:18). To these two individuals interested in eternal life, we can add billions more who still ask the same question today. Realizing the importance of the yearning, the Bible has clearly stated: "For God so loved the world that He gave His one and only Son, that whosoever believes in Him shall not perish but have eternal life" (John 3:16-17). So to all those who have expressed or just felt this yearning, here is the answer: Jesus Christ, who declared, "I am the bread of life, he who comes to me will never go hungry, and he who believes in me will never be thirsty" (John 6:35). He also declared: I am the resurrection.

Eternal life does not consist of having and holding, but in giving and providing for the have-nots, here now on the planet earth. Such life will later transfer to the place where the followers of Jesus move to after they are pronounced biologically dead. Living eternally is being with Christ, being where God is. Yearning for eternal life is essentially yearning for life itself. This is why as we said earlier, St Augustine said: " Our hearts are restless until they rest in thee, O God."

Finally, evangelism is important because it proclaims that which humanity yearns. The gospel we preach is Christ who said, "I am the way, the truth and the life." Those who believe in Jesus Christ, though they die, yet they shall have eternal life.

Three
THE CORNERSTONE OF EVANGELISM

Effective evangelism has a four-fold cornerstone: God, the Bible, the Risen Christ, and the Holy Spirit. We must first turn to God as one of the components that decolonizes the soul. Then as we will discuss the Bible which was written "that they may believe that Jesus Christ is the Saviour," then the Risen Christ and the Holy Spirit. These four are inseparable in the work of evangelism.

I. GOD IN AFRICAN TRADITIONAL RELIGION.

God is the cornerstone of evangelism because He is the Alpha and Omega, the Creator and finisher of history. As Creator of the universe, the whole earth is full of His glory. Africans have known this God through God's own self-revelation since He is spirit.

What Africans believed was confirmed later by Jesus when in a face to face evangelism, He told the Samarian woman at the well that "God is spirit and His worshippers must worship in spirit and in truth," (John 4:24). One of the most incredible things about African Traditional belief in God, is the belief that not only is God Spirit, but He is also a "Spirit Person" with whom worshippers can converse. So God is anthropomorphized by traditionalists. They talk about the Creator in terms of His Eye, His Ear, or His Hand. They believe that He is a living being who is interested in their welfare. In fact, serious scholars of African religion have argued that traditionalists never made or worshipped idols or images of God. They all worship God through their ancestors.

Regarding God in Africa, Professor Gwinyai Muzorewa, a Systematic Theologian, says "...based on scholarly studies as well as empirical evidence, there is every reason to believe that Africans have known and acknowledged the Supreme being, or the ultimate reality from time immemorial," (Muzorewa, 2004 A.2). Another scholar, Dr. E Bolaji Idowu of West Africa supports Dr. Muzorewa's position when he says: "There is no place, age, or generation which did not receive at some point in its history some form of revelation, " (Idowu, 1994, 140).

Africans have various names for God based on whatever manifestation they may have experienced. Of course the names were according to the ethnic languages and regions -- hence the wide range of names. For example "in Southern Africa the Ultimate Reality may be known as *Unkulunkulu*, which literally translates to "the greatest one of the great." Other names include *Inkosi, Nyadenga* and *Ngai*. The Shona of Zimbabwe may call God by trilogy which also expresses some attributes of God: *Muwanikwa, Mutangakugara* and *Chidzachepo*. They also call Him *Mwari*. Incidentally, Christian Zimbabweans also call God by the same traditional name that the Shona speaking people use, *Mwari*. In West African regions, God is known by names like, *Chuku, Olodumare* and *Nyame* to mention a few. In Central and East Africa names like, *Mungu, Bwana, Leza, Nzambi*, are common (Ibid).

The God of traditional Africans has revealed Himself in many forms and is worshipped in different ways. The most dramatic and pragmatic divine manifestation to the best of my knowledge is the famous *Muti usina zita*, literally translated, " the tree without a name." Oral tradition has it that under a certain tree, which is actually located near Waddilove Mission in Marondera District, our ancestors used to worship according to their custom. Following the ritual asking, food would appear in plates and people would eat to their hearts' content. After they had feasted, the wooden plates would be taken away mysteriously to some "dishwasher," until the next meal! No take-aways, carryouts or doggy bags were allowed. (It is possible there are other *Miti isina zita* (pl) in other districts, e.g. Buhera.)

A lot of people who call themselves modernists - - both African and non-Africans - - have dismissed this tradition as, impossible, unrealistic, "nonsense." Well, they are duly entitled to their thinking. As for me, I believe that God can do what He wants to do to save and nurture His people. Furthermore I believe that He is not fenced in some part of the world such that He cannot interact with other communities. So God the Provider who gave the Children of Israel manna from heaven in the wilderness (Ex. 16:4-5), could be the very same God the Provider doing the same wonders at multiple locations in Zimbabwe alone -- not to mention elsewhere. Consequently, the same God of the wilderness who was with Moses and the Israelites is the very One who fed the Africans of long, long ago with the local diet under the tree as we have already stated. And He still sustains them today -- when famine or an epidemic strikes. Yes, God is spirit. He is Omnipresent, Omnipotent and Omniscient and He reveals Himself to different people in various forms although often times people do not acknowledge His presence or give Him credit for what He does for them.

In sum, the God of Abraham, Isaac, Jacob and Father of Jesus Christ is the same who revealed His divinity to the African traditionalists. Like the Biblical God, the God known to and worshipped in traditional Africa is Spirit while at the same time His acts are tangible.

Not Ancestral Worship

African traditionalist have never worshipped ancestors, however, they revere them, knowing that they too are creatures who once worshipped the same Creator God --Unkulunkulu, Mwari, Chuku! Please note that some Africans, out of sheer ignorance or pride or simply theological and cultural confusion seem to believe that African traditionalists worship their living-dead. This is erroneous thinking. My parents were first generation Christians and they associated with traditionalists. Their accounts that I am drawing from are very reliable. This is what happened; when traditionalists had a petition they followed certain protocol: the youngest of the ancestors was asked to pass on the petition to the elder, and this to the oldest group of ancestors[3]. Beyond that point, they would then ask that the oldest ancestor, (in Shona) *"Pfuudzai kuna Musika vanhu."* (Literally, "Pass our petition to the Creator of humanity").

That traditionalists worship God through their ancestors does not mean that their prayers take longer to get to Him because God is Omnipresent and Omniscient. Moreover, God's foreknowledge does not depend on information given. In fact, there is no such thing as "indirect" or "direct" prayer. If Abraham's prayer to God took longer than St. Paul's then the prayer of the traditionalists probably take longer than that of the Christian. But is that plausible? No. Furthermore, most Christians offer their prayers to God through Jesus Christ and they believe that their prayers are heard instantly by God. People who talk in terms of "direct and indirect" need to be reminded that no matter how close, physically, one is to their caller, a cell phone call still has to go through the satellite system even if the person being called is standing right next to the caller. The bottom line is, prayer to God is always a 'direct call' because He has direct link with us and we to Him.

Evangelising among the traditionalist today is relevant and providential because they already believe in God -- the Father of Jesus Christ. Granted they did not know Jesus Christ. Our mere challenge is to simply introduce the Saviour, Jesus, to these God-fearers.

The God of Traditional Africa also insisted upon much of what we have in the Ten Commandments originally given to Moses. For example: don't steal, don't commit adultery, don't kill, don't covet, honour your parents, be in harmony with neighbours, and honour *Chisi* (a holy day of rest). Christianity should find it helpful to preach the resurrection among traditionalists because traditionalists also believe very strongly in "life after death." The doctrine and phenomenon of the Holy Spirit is similar to spirit possession of persons by one's ancestors in the quest to make them a healer or herbalist.

Missionaries who came to evangelise need to know that in Africa they came to introduce Jesus Christ to people who already worship Mwari, the Creator, and Father -- God.

II. THE BIBLE

Evangelism that decolonizes the soul starts with declaring the reign of God -- the God of Africa -- who is also the God of Jesus Christ. The God whose word is recorded in the book we call the Holy Bible, is the Ruler of the Universe. He created Adam and Eve, giving them dominion over all the earth (Gen. 1:26-27), blessed them (Gen. 1:28), and said about His creation " ...it was very good" (Gen. 1:31). This is the same God who seeks to save His own creation. God was

---

[3] In the ritual of ancestor veneration, there is no sexist language even though some ancestors are female, others male.

pleased with His creation especially with humanity whom He created in His own image. So God seeks to redeem us when we are alienated through sin. God does not will that His creation should perish. His will is declared in the Bible.

Unfortunately the first parents of humanity disobeyed God (Gen. 3:6-8) and fell from grace. Thus the crisis of righteousness had started. By sinning they entered a spiritual and moral wilderness. Put simply, they were lost. Eve blamed her disobedience on the serpent which Jesus would later call "Satan" (Luke 10:18). Adam's excuse was that Eve offered him forbidden fruit. So they both sinned. Knowing the way of the tempter, Jesus simply dismissed Satan in the desert, "Away from me Satan!" (Matt. 4:10). Peter also called this ungodly evil spirit "the Devil" (1 Pet. 5:8). The Bible alerts us: "Be sober, be vigilant; because the devil walks about like a roaring lion, seeking whom he may devour." It is surprising that in spite of all this fore-warning, many still fall into temptation.

Adam and Eve, seized with fear, guilt and shame, tried to escape from the presence of God. The Bible says they hid themselves somewhere in the Garden of Eden. How did God respond to this? As always, God responded with love, concern, and desire to redeem them from sin. "Adam. Adam. Where are you?" (Gen. 3:9). In this book, we have chosen this to be the benchmark for the beginning of evangelism. Seeking the lost "while they are yet sinners," is the mission of evangelism. In this sense, God Himself started the ministry of evangelism, but later He would call somebody to do the work.

In the New Testament, the Book of Acts is replete with evangelistic ministry. Furthermore, all four gospels announce repentance, redemption and rebirth. Back to the Old Testament we see that God called Abram, " to go to the land that I will show you" (Gen. 12:1) and all people will be "blessed through you." Moses too was called through the burning bush (Ex 3:2) and was commissioned to bring the children of Israel out of bondage so they might "worship God." (Ex 3:12). In Genesis and Exodus the people of Israel were not only literally politically decolonized and set free to serve God but were also spiritually liberated to serve Him. When God said, "Whom shall I send? And who will go for us?" (Is. 6:8), Isaiah's positive response came after he had experienced spiritual decolonization.

These examples in the Bible demonstrate that God calls persons and sends them on missions. The case of Jeremiah (Jer. 1:5-10) is a beautiful example of purposeful evangelism. To Jonah, God said "Go to the city of Nineveh and preach against it because its wickedness has come up before me," (Jonah 1:2). Clearly, evangelism is God' s initiative and the Bible is the record of such activity. While Jonah was sent to a foreign people, the prophet Ezekiel was sent to Israel: "Son of man, these men have set up idols in their hearts and put wicked stumbling blocks before their faces…Therefore speak to them and tell them. (Ezek 14:3-4). " This is what the Lord says, 'Repent!' Turn from your idols and renounce all your detestable practices!" (Ezek 14:6). God continued to battle with disobedient Israel. Because He does not like to see them dwell in that state of life, God declares that He is pleased when they turn from their wicked ways and live (Ezek 18:23). Right through the book of Ezekiel, the overall motif is evangelistic ... seeking the lost, redeeming the sinners, God reclaiming His own children.

Perhaps one of the most telling of God's evangelistic love is expressed in Hosea. " Then the Lord said to me, 'Go again, love a woman who is loved by a lover and is committing adultery, just like the love of the Lord for the children of Israel, who look to other gods and love the raisin cakes *of the pagans*. So I bought her for myself for fifteen shekels of silver, and one half homers of barley," (Hosea 3:1-2). We need to take the greatest care and observe that, through and through, evangelism is effective when it emanates from God's love and God's forgiveness of sin, rather than our strategy to merely increase membership, or to show the world how sinful it is. Evangelists don't go to sinners to condemn but to introduce them to the God of love who is the only one who can forgive sin. The God who forgives also commands us to love and forgive, even what seems like unforgivable sin. In Isaiah, God says, " Though your sins are like scarlet, they shall be as white as snow, though they are as red as crimson, they shall be like wool," (Isaiah 1:18). The invitation is "come now let us reason together, " (Is. 1:18a). This is God's will revealed to us in the Bible. Regarding the importance of the Bible, we agree with scholars like J.I. Parker who says, "... the basic Biblical perspective is that evangelism is a work of God. God the Creator, in the Glory and power of His unity is both God the redeemer and God the evangelist," (In Hunter III, 1987, 15).

The Bible tells us that whenever God's laws are broken, whether by an individual, groups or nations, God shows Himself in the power of correction. Such was the dramatic case of the beloved King David who was caught in double sin when first he committed adultery with Bathsheeba (2 Sam 11:4) and further on arranged the death of her husband, Uriah, a soldier in his own army (2 Sam. 11:14-15). Obviously, David was totally absorbed in sin -- he was completely bound by the chains of evil. Then God sent Nathan to deliver him from bondage.

Committed evangelists are like prophets. They dare to preach even to the mighty famous and strong, like King David. For the prophet Nathan to say "You are the man." (2 Sam. 12:7) right to the face of The King, must have called for courage. Convicted with the Holy Spirit, David then said: "I have sinned against the Lord" (2 Sam. 12:13). If Nathan or any other prophet had feared to confront him, King David would have died in sin. Today's pastors and preachers who call themselves messengers of God must, in the name of justice confront governments and their leaders that are actually harassing and oppressing their own people through various undemocratic measures under the guise of "independence" and sovereignty.

So where are the prophets? They are everywhere. There are men and women around us, both laity and clergy who are committed servants of God at the expense of being ridiculed, ostracized and even labelled "enemies". I believe that each Christian man and woman, is the custodian of the liberating gospel during their lifetime. Jesus said He was sent "... to release the oppressed." (Luke

4:18) One is tasked to speak and preach the truth that shall "set us free from a variety of self-imposed bondages… It is our business and duty as the custodian of the gospel to lead all persons including national leaders to repentance. The Bible is replete with incidents where God sends men and women to evangelise. There is power in the Word "… Thus says the Lord…" " It is written…" Evangelism which is not biblically based is like a government without a constitution! However, when coupled with the Bible, evangelism is the person, life and work of Jesus Christ.

III. THE RISEN CHRIST

There is no name like Jesus in heaven or on earth. I remember during the 1950's when I directed evangelism at the Annual Conference level in the United Methodist Church in Zimbabwe (then Rhodesia), a young man was stunned by the name JESUS. We met at Bromley, where both of us were waiting to board a train to the nation's capital, Salisbury (now Harare). This train station was devoid of any comfort or amenities but we had to endure the discomfort while waiting for the train. We soon exhausted all polite topics that two strangers could engage in to pass the time. I learned that this immigrant worker was from Mozambique (judging from his accent), and had found a job in Salisbury where he lived with his brother. I waited for an opportunity to introduce *the* topic which, for me, was a matter of spiritual life and death -- *Jesus!* I had been aching to introduce *the* topic from the moment I spotted him.

As the conversation was waning, I asked him point blank: " Do you know Jesus Christ?" Stunned he paused for a moment with a perplexed look. Perhaps he was pondering the question. He responded with a blunt question seeming to beg clarification, yet displaying ignorance, "Does He live in Salisbury?" I immediately concluded, based on his response that this young man did not *know* Jesus and he had never heard of Him. Apparently, I was in the company of someone to whom Jesus was a total stranger. There is no name like it in heaven or earth! However through his response-question, the Lord had presented me with an ample chance to briefly tell this man who Jesus *is*. What an opportunity for *umbowo*/testimony.

The young man listened in silence as I explained how Jesus was born, lived, served and was crucified, died and was buried. Although both of us were listening for the train whistle, I got his undivided attention when I said this Jesus rose from death. "He rose again?" he enquired with utmost surprise. "Yes" I said. "Moreover, He is here with us now in spirit. Even though we can not see Him, He can see us and hear us. I can talk to Him now." I immediately started to pray in such a manner that this young man could realize that I was talking to Jesus. Then I asked him to say something to Jesus too, if he wanted to. So, he too prayed.

There was a dead silence following this prayer session. We were both in deep reflection. Heaven knows what he was thinking! For me, this was one more work of the Holy Spirit who convicts and saves the lost souls. When he finally broke the silence, it was to announce: "Sir, when I get to the city, I want to tell my brother about this Jesus. Also, when I feel lonely, I will talk to Him." In hindsight, I missed the opportunity to baptize him.

Is this not how Christianity was spread by the early church? Those who accepted Jesus witnessed to others -- often, one person at a time, sometimes one family at a time and other times one community at a time (John 4:28-30). My experience has been that the mention of 'Jesus' always triggers a response -- sometimes a curious response! And always, interesting events follow, even if our human eyes cannot see the events immediately. There is power, wonder-working power in the name Jesus Christ. But there is more to the name.

A. Who is Jesus?

According to the Bible, Jesus is the Son of God, and has always been with God. "He was with God in the beginning" (John 1:2). John the Baptist introduced Him to the crowd that was waiting to be baptized in the river Jordan, as "the lamb of God who takes away the sins of the world" (John 1:29). Further, St. John the gospel writer says: "I have seen and testified that this is the Son of God" (John 1:34). In terms of His person and nature, the orthodox faith describes Jesus as both fully human and fully divine. Only He is the Saviour of the world due to His unique nature and purpose. There is something unique about the nature, work and person of Christ. At conception, God said His name shall be called Jesus because He is the saviour of the world. So, Jesus is the Christ, the Saviour, the Son of God, the Lamb of God, the ransom for many, and more.

At Caesarea Philippi, when Jesus asked the question: " Who do people say I am?" Peter's response was, "You are the Christ" (Mark 8:29), the son of the Living God (Mark 8:27). To this confession, Jesus confided that a person could only know Him when this fact is so revealed. Knowing Jesus is not academic; it is not only cognitive but spiritual as well. There is no other like Him in heaven and on earth. Jesus is also unique in that He is a gift to the world, in addition to being its saviour. God gave Jesus to the world; and the world that knows Him must offer Jesus to the rest.

B. Jesus Christ the Son of God Whom We must Offer to the World

Since evangelism started with God, it is reasonable to conclude that the God of Jesus who is also fully divine is God who evangelises. We must keep reminding missionaries and those who sent them that even before the first missionaries arrived on the continent, Africa knew and worshipped God before the distinctions between Father, Son and the Holy Spirit were revealed .

I shall never forget the day when during an evangelistic campaign a lay leader and I visited Chitenderano, one of the local churches. In this area lived an unchurched woman who was in her 90's. Our evangelistic approach was to visit this woman because she did not know Jesus and yet she was a religious person. She obviously was a traditionalist. On this visit we simply said to her: *"Mbuya*

(Granny), we know you worship God. But we have come to tell you that He has a Son called Jesus Christ who died but after three days rose again. His spirit is here."[4]

This approach struck a chord with her because Africans have long believed in life after death. It was nothing new to most spiritually mature Africans, especially one of her age. So, as we conversed with her, she started clapping her hands in the characteristic rhythm that has been used for ages when addressing and praising the Creator. She immediately accepted Jesus and was baptized. Unfortunately, after a few months she died. But the good news was that she had accepted Christ. Effective evangelism does not seek to condemn but to embrace with God's agape love. But for the unchurched to accept Christ, they must hear the gospel preached; they must accept it as offered.

C. Jesus is the Saviour of the World

One more peculiarity with Jesus is that He is " the expiation of our sin." John introduced Him accordingly, "Behold, the lamb of God who takes away the sins of the world" (John 1:29). How does this happen? Does He do that, really?

In the African culture many know that a lamb is one of the most harmless creatures on earth. Also it has been used as the expiation of sin…in cases of forgiveness, peace and reconciliation. Paul would say if a person is in Jesus Christ, he is a new creature (Gal 6:15). So, who is this Jesus who makes "all things new" (Rev 21:5)? Who is this Jesus who has the power to decolonize persons? It is interesting to note that one does not have to be Christian to recognize Jesus.

For instance, the Samaritan woman looked at Jesus and called Him a "prophet": "I can see you are a prophet" (John 4:19). Demons also recognized Jesus as the Son of God (James 2:19). The Centurion was surprised to see what happened when Jesus died hanging on the cross and remarked: "Surely He was the Son of God" (Matt. 27:54) (Mark 15:39). When Saul of Tarsus was struck from his horse, even though he was evil and opposed to Christ, he suddenly called out, "Lord!" It is fair to say that these people recognized Jesus even though they did not accept Him as "their saviour" initially. By the same token, Jesus may know more people than those who call themselves Christians. After all, as the Saviour of the whole world, that is within His purview.

D. Jesus is the Light of the World

Jesus declares, " I am the light of the world. Whoever follows me will never walk in darkness, but will have the light of life (John 8:12). I have come to the world as a light, so that no one who believes in me should stay in darkness"

---

[4] By the way, evangelising African traditionalists is relatively easy because of the African belief in God who is Spirit and is always present among us. Evangelising is meaningful among people of African decent because it is a matter of adding the name Jesus to the belief in God. In accepting Jesus, African traditionalists have nothing to lose but everything to gain really.

(John 12:46). " While I am in the world, I am the light of the world (John 9:5). Darkness is definitely hovering over the earth. It shows its ugly head in broad daylight as what Paul called principalities ... of fear, demon possession, superstition, witchcraft, oppression, racism, terrorism, war, sexism and ignorance. This darkness is manifesting itself not only in Africa but even in so called developed regions of the world. The result is the sickening statistics of immorality ranging from abortion to homosexuality. We also see the results of this darkness in church decline among main line denominations where Satan moves angel-like on the wings of modernism, scientific and popular culture, and in the worship of various gods called materialism.

It pains me to see how the African people still suffer and die from fear, ignorance and superstition over and above the ravaging pandemic disease which itself was caused by promiscuity and general spiritual disharmony. It reminds me of the prophet who said: "My people die from lack of knowledge" (Hosea 4:6). If only everyone, everywhere, not just in Africa, had the light of Jesus Christ. I know this to be true because I have seen and witnessed what a difference it makes. I have witnessed every form of wickedness transformed to kindness and consideration for others. I have witnessed people and communities transformed in many glorious ways once the light of Jesus Christ touched them.

For example, about 22 miles (35 kilometres) south of Mutare, Zimbabwe's eastern border- town, lies a place once condemned, even by its name *"Dambakurimwa."* [It means a place that refuses to be ploughed or farmed.] Such was its condemnation, for without ploughing there can never be any harvest. In this area was a superstition that if anyone dared even attempt to till the land, some unknown dire consequence would befall them, most likely untimely death. For a very long time, the inhabitants of this area had lived in poverty due to fear of the unspecified, and had gone hungry while this land was idle, yet God had given them such fertile land.

One man who accepted Jesus dismissed the superstition and had his "spiritual eyes" opened by His light. Maxen Mutambanengwe, who attended primary school at Old Mutare Mission Centre, challenged his superstitious community. A born again Christian, he was free from fear, ignorance and superstition, and so one summer, during the school holidays, he cleared a piece of virgin land, and planted crops. Amidst the outcry and bitter criticism of the Dambakurima community, he had a bumper harvest. The community was so certain evil would befall him, but nothing happened to him. Seeing no evil befalling him, others began to follow suit after a while. The light from a single individual had spread to the family, to the community and it spread throughout the region. Jesus the Light wants us to be "...the light of the world" (Matt. 5:14). Those who walk in the light will bring light to others.

There are numerous examples of this kind. In fact the light of Jesus has shone on Africa so long now that we can no longer regard the continent as the seat of darkness. Most regions of Africa are now a shining example even in some areas that used to be an eyesore. This has come through the general evangelism initially introduced by missionaries. Before the Zimbabwean war of liberation,

95% of schools were run by churches. Christian schools in Africa in general and Zimbabwe in particular, believe it is their duty to preach the gospel to their students. Consequently, many graduates of these schools are Christians. In Africa South, 65% of Africa is now baptized Christians. Some label themselves as "born again." Couples married by traditional customs are choosing to take vows afresh in church because they have learned that "a Christian marriage" has more spiritual values than the others do. Some governments, e.g. South Africa, allow Christians to worship even in secular situation such as funerals of government officials. Women have taken their place in centre stage in pulpits, the judiciary and business. However, in spite of this ray of light, there is still need for the Word to be preached. Hence the need to evangelise. The very best that has ever happened to Africa is that Jesus who liberates the oppressed and lightens the world was introduced to the continent! Praise God!

E. The Ultimate Miracle: The Empty Tomb

The resurrection of Christ, more than His birth and miracles, is one of the most cardinal beliefs in world religions' debate today. Did Jesus really rise from the dead? The resurrection of Christ makes him a very unique founder. Other founders lived and died, but Jesus lives eternally. Thus, there is no other like Him.

The story goes that two people were arguing: a Moslem and a Christian. Each defined the merits of his faith. They compared the histories of each and their respective advantages. After a long debate, the two sides were evenly matched -- point for point. Finally they compared the practices. The Moslem said, "We are not like you Christians who travel all the way to Jerusalem to visit an empty tomb. When we go to Mecca we find our leader Muhammad's tomb neatly intact, just as he was buried." At that point the Christian jumped up with enthusiasm, pride and joy and said "Got you! And herein is the difference. Our Jesus rose from the dead. He is not dead in the tomb. He is living today. His presence is experienced in many parts of the world. So is our Christian religion. It is not a dead faith." This historical fact killed the argument and terminated any further discussion.

F. The Resurrection

The Bible tells us that Jesus rose from the dead. The women who followed Jesus throughout His ministry before He was crucified, went to try and anoint His body with oil according to Jewish customs but they could not because His body was not there. Worse still, they could not find Him. Instead they saw an angel that consoled them: " Do not be afraid, for I know that you are looking for Jesus who was crucified. He is not here. He has risen, just as He said." (Matt. 28:5-6) (Mark 16:6-7). Late that day Cleopas and his companion were going to a village called Emmaus. Jesus accompanied them incognito. They talked with this third person and they even ate with Him (Luke 24:13-35) but did not know it was Jesus. Later He appeared to His disciples and others assembled in Jerusalem (Luke 24:33) where Cleopas and his companion reported their experience with the risen Lord. The Scriptures have sufficient data about His resurrection. What is left for each heart to have enough faith that Jesus was raised from the dead. The appeal in this book is, those who believe that Jesus Christ is Lord must "go and teach, baptizing in the name of the Father, the Son and Holy Spirit." In a word, E-V-A-N-G-E-L-I-Z-E because He lives!

G. We worship the risen Lord!

Mary preached the very first sermon ever preached after Jesus rose from the dead! Congratulations women of God! She declared, " I have seen the Lord" (John 20:18). That Mary saw the evidence of the resurrection, is stated in the Bible which is our textbook for evangelism written so that we may believe. Jesus told Thomas, "Blessed are those who have not seen and yet have believed" (John 20:24). The Bible is not a science handbook. It is a collection of witnesses and instruction, not "proofs."

Every community on earth looks back into its history and identifies a day or period that they remember as the worst day of their history -- its darkest hour. In the Christian community Good Friday, the day Jesus was crucified, is the worst day and the best day at once. The disciples had all their hopes dashed and some were surely in hiding. Their hearts were filled with fear of the Jews and the Romans alike. On the day of the crucifixion they had nothing much to look forward to. The future was bleak and only darkness loomed ahead. Their mission to illuminate 'the way' for others had died a sudden death, they thought.

In the early days the apostles and disciples would refer to Christianity as "The Way." But when Jesus was crucified they must have felt there was 'no way' forward anymore. Things were really terrible if not downright dangerous. It is a wonder this is the day we recognize as "Good" Friday. They may never have found a way had the Christ not risen. Perhaps it might only have ended up as merely a small circle of fishermen meeting occasionally to reminisce about what might have been -- a sort of club of former followers.

But He rose from the dead! That made all the difference. In the emptiness of the tomb is the fullness of the message that Jesus rose. The point here is that God makes *the way* out of no way. The crucifixion and the death of Jesus did not stifle God's plan to save humanity. In fact, it actually facilitated it. So yes, Jesus is the Way, the truth and the life.

Today we speak of Good Friday because the atonement made it good. If Christ had not undergone the most ignominious death and the atonement, there would have been no glorious resurrection. The horror of the crucifixion was reversed and transformed by God's power and grace. Christ's death became our life. Without the resurrection our Christian faith would have been buried forever. So in effect the resurrection couched the concept of the Jesus of eternal life. The resurrection further signifies that geography or biology does not limit Jesus, who conquered death. The resurrection gives us a universal Christ, a victorious Prince of Peace.

H. Mary Magdalene To Lydia Chimonyo

One of the most glorious and dynamic entities in the United Methodist Church in Zimbabwe is in *Rukwadzano rwe Wadzimai (RRW)* (the United Methodist Women's Fellowship) I want to call it a movement or organization but neither one does true justice to its spirit-centred dynamism. Bishop Eben Nhiwatiwa called it "... the powerhouse in the United Methodist Church in spiritual and material terms",in his book *The Humble Beginnings* (Nhiwatiwa p. 106). I shudder to think what the United Methodist Church in Zimbabwe would be like without it. For anyone to narrate how it started, one will have to talk about the work of the Holy Spirit. Here I simply want to share s testimony about Lydia as a specially anointed leader[5].

Briefly, it happened that Lydia, wife of Obediah Chimonyo, then a seminarian at Old Mutare, went to look for *tsenza* (an edible root) and to visit Manyarara, a church station behind the Chiremba Mountain. While she and other women were there, they learned that there was going to be a revival church service that afternoon at a nearby local Methodist Church. Though they were tired from the nearly 14 mile (22.5 kilometres) journey, they decided to attend the service. Following the sermon, there was an altar call as usual. Lydia started jumping up and down shouting at the top of her voice. "I have seen Jesus! I have seen Jesus!" In some parts of the world they would have tied her up and taken her off to a psychiatrist. Thank God she was among people of 'The Way' who understood that it is not only possible but normal to see a spiritual body, even when others do not see it. Saul of Tarsus did also on the road to Damascus (Acts 9:1-f). Moses was called by God (Ex. 3:6). In the same manner Jesus had appeared to this devout woman. This is the same resurrected Jesus that Mary Magdalene saw in the Garden when she proclaimed to the disciples and others that she had seen the Lord (John 20:18). A spiritual sisterhood had been established between Mary Magdalene and Lydia Chimonyo; she had seen the one and same Jesus who appeared to some of the disciples at the appointed place. This is the same Christ who said to the disciples: " Peace be with you" and showed them His wounded hands and sides. This is the same Christ whom they then reported to the Doubting Thomas: "We have seen the Lord" (John 20:25). This is the Jesus who, centuries later, revealed Himself to Lydia (*Duri, Soko Mukanya*[6]) Chimonyo. **I believe Christ lives today in His Spiritual body.**

Following this encounter with Jesus, Lydia and other women decided to go to this nearby mountain at Old Mutare, at 4 a.m. to pray. The place has since become the sacred open-air sanctuary for the RRW. Since then it has been the

---

[5] I fully recognize the ministry to women, Women Foreign Mission Society and Women Conference which existed before the RRW existed in Zimbabwe. I accepted the claim by RRW that Lydia Chimonyo started their organization probably before "...this early committee." (Nhiwatiwa p.97) of three women of which Lydia was a member. It was informal and on a low key operating in the stations.

[6] Totem designations signifying utmost respect in our Shona culture.

practice for women within walking distance to go to the *Chingando* for prayer every Friday and Sunday for *Rumuko* (a sunrise service). Individuals or groups are welcome. All over the Conferences of Zimbabwe, women go for *Rumuko* services in their churches. At times women travel from the four corners of the country to spend time in prayer at *Chingando* -- the birth place of the United Methodist women's organization in Zimbabwe. Many have laid their burden down at the *Chingando* and have witnessed answered prayers. Furthermore, as Mary Magdalene and others went to the tomb before sunrise on the day of the resurrection so the women of Zimbabwe express their spiritual commitment to Jesus through *Rumuko*.

Incidentally, women of other denominations throughout Southern Africa are also following the footsteps of Mary Magdalene. Different denominations now proudly wear various uniforms of coordinated colours representing their denomination as they share this faith -- that Jesus rose from the dead and He lives today within our hearts. In all this the Holy Spirit guides and teaches them to be more faithful to their Lord and Saviour.

I. Personal Experiences with Jesus Christ

It has been said "Experience is the best teacher." Without doubt to be effective in evangelism, one needs to have personal experience with Jesus Christ. That is where the power of evangelism resides. Some of the apostles said: " We talk of what we heard and saw" (1 John 1:1). Effective evangelism is based on knowing Jesus Christ as one's Lord and Saviour. Knowing Jesus in this sense is not just an academic articulation of the nature, work and person of Jesus Christ. I don't have to tell anyone that we don't go to seminaries to look for the Holy Spirit. We go only to learn how to structure our thinking and expression of the faith. Most of all one goes to seminary to learn how to articulate their faith experiences -- what we have in our life -- our "burning bush," our "strangely warmed hearts" and "Damascus Road experiences," as it were. Effective evangelism is based on one's personal experience with Jesus. In Paul's ministry, he does not dwell on his university and Gamaliel time. Rather he drives his point home very effectively when he tells people how he met Jesus on the way to Damascus, his personal experience! I believe our personal experience with Jesus Christ of Nazareth who is encountered in almost every nation, is a very crucial component of effective evangelism.

IV. THE HOLY SPIRIT

The 1918 Pentecost in Zimbabwe

The power of the Written Word and Jesus' power is manifested in the work of the Holy Spirit, which is the fourth aspect of the cornerstone of evangelism. But who is this Holy Spirit? Or rather, what is the Holy Spirit? Almost all African preachers count on the interceding power of the Holy Spirit when they preach, because the Holy Spirit is God whom they preach. In Trinitarian language, the Holy Spirit is the Third Person of Trinity. He is God. And since the Son is also God, there is a sense in which the Holy Spirit is inseparable from Jesus Christ who once walked in Palestine. This is especially so in light of the Incarnation. Jesus was in the Spirit. In His human form, He taught, preached, ate, wept and performed miracles in Spirit. After resurrection, the Lord still does His work of saving but now in His spiritual form. Furthermore, the Holy Spirit has the personality and character of Jesus Christ. Both are persons. Both speak "to the church" (Rev. 2:7) "... the Holy Spirit said, set apart for me Barnabas and Saul for the work to which I have called them" (Acts 13:2). He ...intercedes with us...(Rom. 8:26). He testifies about Jesus (John 15:26). He can be grieved. "... do not grieve the Holy Spirit of God, with whom you were sealed for the day of redemption" (Eph 4:30). He can be blasphemed. However, to distinguish the two the Bible says "...every sin and blasphemy will be forgiven men, but the blasphemy against the Holy Spirit will not be forgiven" (Matt. 12:31-32).

In an African context, it is quite easily understood that Jesus is in the spiritual body because as pointed out earlier, Africans have long believed in life after death -- their ancestors concept. We still believe that at the end of life on earth people do not actually die, rather they simply leave the earthly body and assume a spiritual one. Traditionalists also believe that the spirit must find a host -- human being -- through whom it can speak. Thus the Holy Spirit is God incarnate when He expresses Himself through a human being, first through the man called Jesus of Nazareth, then through a host of others like St. Paul, St Peter, Lydia Chimonyo, David Mandisodza, Conrad Chigumira, Martha Mudzengerere, Rudo Bingepinge, Kingston Kahlari, Elisha Kabungaidze, Phillip Mupindu, Faith Nyagato, *Evangelist* Kamupira, and all those who have ever been filled and/or refilled with the Holy Spirit. However, this does not mean the Holy Spirit can only manifest Himself through the human body. As God He can do anything He chooses.

When I was a young lay pastor, I was stationed at Mutoko, (Nyadiri East Circuit). During one of my very first worship services there, at Gwenambira, a young girl, not more than 14 years old, was attacked by an evil spirit, a demon[7]. It is not clear when the demon possessed her, but what was evident is the demon was no longer comfortable living in her. I saw with my own eyes how she was transformed into a giant in terms of her physical strength. Imagine as many as five well built men plus a muscular woman tried to restrain her and pin her down but she would flex and toss the lot of them off her at will. Apparently when a person is possessed by a demon, the individual is totally transformed. One becomes really wild. I was shocked and surprised to see this. It was an eye

---

[7] There is a difference between being demon possessed and being possessed by an ancestor's spirit. An ancestor's spirit seeks to heal while demon possession seeks destruction! Of course there are times when the ancestors punish the living for immoral acts. Furthermore, the ancestors choose to possess a loved, chosen member of their living family, not just anybody.

opener to see a human being in the state of being possessed by a demon. I had often heard stories, some of them very graphically told, but I had never witnessed it. There it was.

Although I am not a traditionalist, I understand how Jesus' spiritual body can be everywhere at once, just as ancestors are experienced as spiritual bodies when they visit the living. So I understand that the resurrected Jesus is all over the world in His spiritual body, which He Himself called "the Holy Spirit" in John 14:17. One understands that Spirit can fill people and give them the power which Jesus had access to in His historical existence. Of course, understanding Jesus' spiritual body is not just confined to Africans. In his book *The Holy Spirit*, Dr. Billy Graham once said: " We accept the fact that the Holy Spirit is God, just in as much as God the Father, God the Son and the Son is also God" (Billy Graham, 1978). Put differently, Christ and the Holy Spirit are inseparably one. Just as the Son and the Father are inseparably one. They work harmoniously as the doctrine of the trinity clearly explains.

Jesus promised to send us the Holy Spirit. "But the counsellor, the Holy Spirit, whom the father will send in my name, will teach you all the things and will remind you of everything I have said to you" (John 14:26). Jesus also promised "... you will receive power when the Holy Spirit comes on you." (Acts1:8) Peter in his sermon on the day of Pentecost said, among other things, "...the promise of receiving the Holy Spirit is for you and your children and for all that are far off who the Lord our God will call" (Acts 2:39). Furthermore, the Holy Spirit was not to be thought of as being confined to the upper room in Jerusalem. What we have on the day of Pentecost is a major manifestation of the Spirit who is present throughout the universe. This is the same Spirit that was hovering on the surface of the void in the beginning (Gen. 1:2). This is consistent with our belief that the Holy Spirit is the third person of the Trinity. Just as we believe God is omniscient, omnipresent and omnipotent, so are the Holy Spirit and Christ. It is no wonder my parents experienced the Holy Spirit at Muziti.

In Zimbabwe, the year 1918 is known as *Gore reMweya Mutsvene* (The year of the Holy Spirit) -- meaning people re-lived the Pentecost in an even dramatic and most amazing manner. I cannot resist the sharing with you some of what happened at this African Pentecost.

The late Rev. John Munjoma and I had the privilege to interview Rev. Luke Chieza, one of UMC clergy pioneers who was present when the Zimbabwe Pentecost occurred. Rev. Luke Chieza was one of the youth lay pastors when the Holy Spirit dramatically filled everybody who was present at the conference. He always related the incident with vivid recollection. From this incident, Rev. Chieza said he learned that the Holy Spirit happens through the preacher and in spite of the preacher! It is not so much what we do as what the Spirit Holy chooses to do among the worshippers. (There may be minor variations on reports as they were given to those who interviewed the eyewitnesses of the day of the Holy Spirit.)

According to Rev. Luke Chieza it was during the morning devotions of the

Annual Conference meeting of lay pastors, which was led by a Baptist guest preacher, Mr. Hatch from Rusitu Mission Centre. He read a passage from Acts Chapter 2 and he began to explain in a soft, calm voice, the promises of the Scriptures, and he posed the rhetorical question: "What can prevent us from receiving the Holy Spirit now?" Then he gave instruction to everybody: "Let us go for a session of quiet personal prayer." The statement seemed to have immediately invoked the Holy Spirit into their midst. God poured the Holy Spirit into the hearts of all the worshippers that day. Strange things began to happen. Right then, in that worship service, some started affirming loudly "Amen! Amen! Amen!" repeatedly. Some wept, some were *laughing* loudly, some where singing, some where jumping up and down, while others ran out of the church building to find a place for quiet individual prayer and meditation, others went to look for people to witness to.

For those who did not know what was happening it was a strange sight indeed. Typically, non- believers concluded everyone was acting crazy! The noise and organized chaos curiously attracted those that were near the little old chapel at Old Mutare, where this originated. I call this "organized" because I believe that God's manifestations are always organized and systematic even though the human eye may not see it as such.

Based on interviews, Nhiwatiwa has this to share about the day of the Holy Spirit at Old Mutare in *The Humble Beginnings*. "Needless to say the conference session was almost disrupted as most delegates went to look for non-believers, in order to preach to them." This is what actually happened at Old Mutare Centre. So we must call it "the Zimbabwe Pentecost."

Now let us compare what happened at these two locations, centuries and thousands of miles apart: on the one hand, the Pentecost of the Upper Room in Jerusalem, Palestine and the Pentecost of the church at Old Mutare, Zimbabwe on the other.

- First, people were gathered waiting and praying, ten to fourteen days at Old Mutare and Jerusalem..
- Secondly, the Scriptures were read.
- An outburst or outpouring of the Holy Spirit occurred.
- Then people acted strangely, "crazily", and were accused of being "drunk".
- Each one went out to witness the power of God in action.
- Those affected were totally transformed and inspired to preach, and evangelise.
- There was "…Phenomenon of fire which when touched did not burn (Nhiwatiwa p 79) and "tongues of fire" Acts 2:3)
- Eighth, sharing miracles was wrought.
- Ninth, the church was resurrected or born again.

This eighth aspect is quite intriguing. Please note that aspects iv through ix all result from aspect iii. However let us focus on this eighth. The result of the outpouring of the Holy Spirit was evangelisation followed by massive conversion and baptisms. Peter preached and 3000 people converted. At Old Mutare, a young lay person, David Mandizodza and his colleague John Cheke walked over 20 miles (32 kilometres) to Chief Mutasa area to preach and baptize. Additionally like Peter and John, who healed a cripple at the gate of the temple called Beautiful, the Zimbabwean counterparts came upon a woman, Dorcas Muredzwa, who was lame and had never walked. They laid hands on her saying "Dorcas, In Jesus' name, you rise up and walk." Dorcas sprang up and shouted: "Friends, I am healed. Jesus Christ has healed me. I am no longer a cripple. Halleluya! Halleluya!" (Nhiwatiwa p.80)

Jesus in a spiritual body is working with us through us and for us. What He did through the first apostles, He is still doing in the world today. He may seem to be a remote power when actually we are the ones distancing ourselves from Him. Jesus in His spiritual body seeks to minister to those in affliction through you and in spite of you. Will you invoke the Holy Spirit -- Jesus' Spirit in you?

Today we recognize that where the Holy Spirit is just given lip service, treated like a joke, archive or museum article, churches and even whole denominations get cold, sick and eventually die. But where the Holy Spirit is given His place, i.e. worshipped, believed in and invoked seriously, congregations have spiritual vitality and growth is evident.

My Personal Pentecost

Allow me to share a personal experience. Some years ago before I retired, my *Sahwira* (ritual friend) and his wife (now late), Rev. Fanuel and Norah Kadenge, were studying in Kentucky, USA. At about time for Annual Conference in Zimbabwe, Fanuel called me from Kentucky to share that he would miss being at Annual Conference since he could not make the long and expensive trip to Zimbabwe. So, he asked me to record some of my morning devotional messages for him to listen to later.

That year the Annual Conference was held at Dadaya Mission, a Church of Christ Centre in Zimbabwe. One of my devotion messages was titled; *"Did You Receive The Holy Spirit When You Were Saved?"* (Acts 19:2). Incidentally, this same question was put to some believers at Ephesus by the apostle Paul during one of his missionary journeys. I believe every generation must at least be confronted by this rhetorical question. Furthermore, one must pray for spiritual renewal always.

Several months later when I travelled to the USA for one of the bi-annual Council of Bishops meeting, I took some of the tapes with me. One morning, we sat at the Kadenge's breakfast table listening to the sermon on *"Did You Receive The Holy Spirit When You Were Saved?"* on tape. Ten minutes or so into the taped message, I felt tears filling my eyes. I looked at Fanuel and his wife through tearful eyes, only to find they too, had tears running down their cheeks. We listened. We sobbed. We Worshipped!

Why did we all get so spontaneously tearful during the playback? If it had been just one of us, I might have crafted some (secular) explanation; however for all of us including the preacher to be touched was beyond my comprehension at the time. For a long time I pondered it and I thought there was no good explanation. But now I think I understand what happened that morning.

Both my friends are deeply spiritual people. I now firmly believe that the Kadenges and I were being refilled with the Holy Ghost of Pentecost, and this is why. Upon further reflection, I later recalled that on the morning when I preached and recorded that message at Dadaya Mission, some clergy and laity, like the late Rev. Chigumira and (then Rev.) Bishop Eben Nhiwatiwa, responded and received spiritual renewal. They went out to seek quiet prayer time. Indeed the proceedings of that morning's Annual Conference business were temporarily postponed, in the same manner the 1918 Conference business had been disrupted at Old Mutare. The Holy Spirit who visited us at Dadaya had visited again in U.S.A. as we listened to the sermon. It still amazes me that the Holy Spirit would visit both (a) at the Annual Conference, such an august event, and (b) at the family breakfast table for just the three of us.

The Holy Spirit Works as Promised.

" And when He has come, He will convict the world of sin, and of righteousness, and of judgment: Of sin because they do not believe in Me: Of righteousness because I go to my Father and you see Me no more: Of judgement, because the ruler of this world is judged." (John 16:8-11).

A. He will convict the world of guilt and sin.

Sometimes I have heard preachers get carried away and overcome with ego saying " I converted so-and-so to come to church." Let it be known, dear reader, that all the evangelists do is to proclaim the word. It is the Holy Spirit who convicts the sinner. Yes, it is the Holy Spirit alone who leads people to repentance!

B. The Holy Spirit teaches.

Have you ever wondered how your mind suddenly opens to new thinking, new ideas, new insights and strategies when confronted with challenges? Have you ever wondered how, when confronted with a challenge you immediately begin to see how you should commit yourself to it? I believe all this is the secret work of the Holy Spirit who teaches, guides and sustains us. In making these claims I am not negating the power of reason, intelligence and all.

C. The Holy Spirit also has the power to "condemn."

He condemns the Prince of the World -- the devil. When one is engaged in evangelism, one is in the heat of a Holy battle with God on one's side -- the power of the Holy Spirit fighting for us and with us, against "the Prince of this world." In order to win the war against evil, every evangelist needs the Holy Ghost Power on his/her side. His main function is to convict as well as empower the saints.

D. The Holy Spirit is a counsellor (John 16: 25).

He tells us what we must or *must not* do if we listen through spiritual ears. Ironically, it is those who know the Holy Spirit who also tend to listen to Him more. For example, in a vision in connection with the segregation and discrimination against Gentiles, "a voice spoke to him (Peter) again the second time, 'What God has cleansed you must not call common,'" (Acts 10:15). The Spirit advised Peter that Gentiles are like any other human beings. They ought to be received as such. Evangelising Gentiles was a major departure and including them in Jesus' body was unheard of, as they were uncircumcised. Based on this new insight, Peter, at the great council in Jerusalem, would argue: "They have received the Holy Spirit just as we have" (Acts 10:47). Furthermore, the Holy Spirit can counsel and lead us to change ourselves, other individuals, congregations, denominations, entire societies, and even governments.

V. CULTURE: INCULTURATION

Culture is a crucial matrix within which the gospel must be planted. Of course every people have their own culture yet the crucial role of culture is either to appropriate the gospel or to destroy it. I believe in the power of culture to shape any given people. For this reason culture is a salient aspect of the foundation for effective evangelism.

As the saying goes, there are two sides to a coin, so is the case with culture. It can strengthen and enrich the precepts of Christianity. Or, it may become a stumbling block to the planting of the faith. Fortunately, the gospel has power to transform any culture when the latter has been presented effectively. It should not be surprising that a tribe that used to be warriors, after accepting Christ, becomes peace-loving; a woman, who used to hate others to the point of being labeled a witch, becomes a caring Christian. The gospel has power to decolonize persons, transforming them from secular to God-loving, and fervent worshippers.

In discussing evangelism, I have selected a few aspects of culture which have become ideal allies of Christianity, *and* a couple others which became foes of the faith because of the call for a radical transformation.

A. The Extended Family Concept

In Chapter One I outlined how the African culture in general impacted on my upbringing; now we look at how one aspect of our culture interacts with Christianity.

The extended family is a remarkably cohesive instrument that creates and provides a very healthy environment for people of African descent. The extended family extends the family horizon beyond the nuclear family. Each member of the nuclear family relates to numerous cousins beyond one's own "immediate" family. For example among the *Shona* people, all cousins are either called *mununguna* (young brothers or sisters) or *mukoma*, (elder brothers or sisters). Therefore, there are always brothers, sisters, mothers and fathers, grandmas and grandpas who love you dearly. This concept of the extended family is an ally of Christianity in that it upholds the concept of sharing, loving, forgiving and even sacrificing. It does not harbour feelings of unhealthy individualism. One always thinks: "I am because we are… and because we are, therefore I am." How can any African ever ask: who am I? The extended family guarantees a sense of belonging which is very critical in human identity. The church ought to embrace such a concept because it enhances togetherness, a sense of security and belonging.

As we pointed out in Chapter One, many people are not in mental institutions because their families are there for them when unemployment, homelessness and loneliness deal their harsh blows. The caring effect of the extended family explains why there are fewer African beggars on the streets than one would expect given the poverty levels. The ageing do not have to dread being stuck with some strangers in the nursing homes because they are invited to live with family. Yes, it costs a lot of money but for Africans human life is more important than money even though one needs money to support family. Family is a form of social security. It is for this reason that traditionally Africans believed in having many children.

Thousands and millions of old people who are not in old peoples' homes live in the homes of their relatives until death removes them. Family assures them of love, care and a continued sense of belonging. The Shona have a saying that enforces the extended family concept: "*Karere, Kanozokurerawo,*" meaning, if you take good care of some orphan, at your old age, the same will take good care of you. At least this is the principle.

In sum, the extended family concept is basically consistent with Christianity. Of course there may be some variations which may be inconsistent, but for the most part, the Christian concept of community finds expression in the extended family. One other very crucial component has to do with the importance of the blood link. In the extended family all are linked through blood or marriage. Therefore, blood-link signifies commitment, connection and a bond, which nothing can ever undo or break, not even death, since the ancestor connection continues beyond death.

B. Life after Death

As we have stated, long before Christianity came to Africa our people believed in life after death. Christianity teaches about the resurrection of the dead and the communion of the saints as articulated in the Apostles' Creed, has a strong connecting link with what Africans' believed traditionally. This parallel provides a firm base for the foundation of the gospel in our culture.

The concept of the communion of the deceased and the living is one of the cultural aspects on which the gospel can be based. For example, that the deceased takes the role of protector, providing security for their living relatives -- relates readily to the guardian angel concept which Christianity teaches. Also,

Masvikiro among the Shona of Zimbabwe, are believed to possess the living person in order to communicate what needs to be known by the living. *Masvikiro* also communicate in dreams. It is not unusual that one is shown a healing herb for a certain illness in a dream. People who still believe cultural manifestations tell us that when they receive instructions in the dream, such instruction is as good as the word of God.

As a matter of fact, there are numerous incidences where God instructed biblical people in dreams. We only need to use them in evangelising the gospel but do not seem to take them seriously when God speaks to us in dreams. In Acts 9:10-19, Saul was instructed by God to go to Ananias who had had a dream about his whole healing scenario. I believe that God can choose to appear to any of us for any particular purpose. Usually, God uses channels already known to the recipient - - such as dreams, visions, revelations, inspiration and so on. How many of us listen when God speaks through any of these cultural modes?

C. Aspects of Culture which Clash with Jesus' Teaching

When Jesus declared: "You have heard that it was said 'Love your neighbour and hate your enemy," (Matt. 5:43), He was using pre-existing laws to build on the fullness of God's law of love. To add on, He says: "But I tell you: Love your enemies and pray for those who persecute you that you may be sons of your Father in heaven." (Matt. 5:44). Jesus also says "You have heard that it was said, eye for an eye, and tooth for tooth; but I tell you... If someone strikes you on the right cheek, turn to him the other also" (Matt. 5:38-39). The point here is that the gospel sometimes clashes with our culture! Our culture taught "eye for an eye" as a law of self-preservation.

Jesus did not go along with what was the religious, moral and ethics of the day, if it was not in line with the love and teachings of God's kingdom. For instance, Jesus emphasized forgiving unconditionally. However, first He understood the Jewish law and its limitations, then He would state God's fullest law of love. The church must present the gospel in such a manner that it either decolonizes the souls, or transforms the whole culture through use of the love of God.

In Zimbabwe, at least among the *Shona*, there is quite an interesting and practical custom on child adoption. It goes like this: if a man was proved to be impotent, but he was desperate to have children, his *"tete"* (aunt, i.e. usage reserved for father's sister) would have a highly confidential conference with his brother, whether younger or older and ask him to sleep with his brother's wife. They would arrange to send the husband to some relative who lived far away -- allowing two or three days to get there and back. Usually this was calculated to coincide with the woman's ovulation period. The child born to this marriage belongs to the family -- extended family -- in every way! The child was never regarded as an adopted one. He or she belonged and was entitled to inheritance like any biological heir. The question of infidelity never came up because this was viewed as a remedy to a hardship in the family.

When Christian marriages were introduced, this way of maintaining the family ties was rendered unchristian because every couple vows to be faithful. The church of Jesus must transform customs that are opposed to Christian principles. But the church must endorse aspects of culture that bless and enrich society. Let us remember that Jesus did not come to condemn or destroy, but to confirm God's love. My wish is that the gospel takes on the local colour so that it transforms not only the individuals but also families and the entire community. I believe that a Christian community is one where everything is done according to how Christ would have it. This is why I believe that culture is an indispensable cornerstone of evangelism when it is consistent with the gospel.

VI. CHRISTIAN EXPERIENCE

John the beloved says, "that which we have heard, which we have seen with our eyes, which we have looked at and our hands have touched this we proclaim concerning the word of life" (1 John 1:1) "...we proclaim to you what we have seen and heard, so that you also may have fellowship with us. And our fellowship is with the Father and with His son, Jesus Christ" (1 John 1:3).

John's point here is that the strength of his words, and the authority with which he speaks comes from the first hand experience. When someone has seen something with his/her own eyes, and heard it with his/her own ears, one has the right to defend the fact. Even if someone were to contest it, the witness would still hold on because in any court of law, an eyewitness is the ultimate. Most people would agree with the position that the most effective witnessing, i.e. the most powerful and moving sermon, comes from someone with integrity who speaks from personal experience. Experience empowers even illiterate people because what they testify is written on their hearts. This is especially the case regarding Christian experience. I know some barely literate persons who preach such powerful sermons that one would assume that the speaker graduated from the school of preaching. Furthermore, many souls are touched and moved even to tears by sermons delivered based on experience. There is tremendous power in personal experience because it is actually one's testimony, which comes from the heart. It also comes out of self-examining questions like: What happened to me? What has God said to me? Has He touched me somehow? When and where? What does the Bible mean to me in relation to Jesus' life and ministry? Have I been blessed? How do I relate to Jesus Christ? Such questions tend to provoke and account for one's life experiences, which make our preaching and teaching effective and productive.

The strength of the Church in Africa today is not based just on what the early missionaries taught about Jesus and Christianity. Rather it is because numerous African Christians have personally experienced the risen and living Christ. I stand with thousands of African Christians who declare: no one and nothing shall separate us from the love of God because we have personally experienced -- tasted and benefited from being believers. This is why Christian experience is regarded as a major aspect of evangelism.

Christian experience has become a tradition in the church. In fact, it is one of the four major sources of Protestant theology, as John Wesley understood it. The Zimbabwean Christians believe because they have seen people who were most wretched sinners repent and converted completely by the saving power of Jesus. Furthermore, we have seen and experienced the wonder working power of the Holy Spirit in our lives. Miracles of healing and other turn of events have convinced us that there is power in the name of Jesus Christ. We have experienced the presence of Jesus of faith among us; we shall cling to God, to Jesus Christ, to the Holy Spirit forever and ever.

Amen!

Four
EVANGELISM THAT DECOLONIZES THE SOUL

I. WHAT EVANGELISM IS NOT

Mere physical features without "life" or "spirit" do not constitute evangelism. In this chapter, the purpose is to define evangelism in such a way that one should be able to diagnose one's own situation either in a local church, a district, Annual Conference or even denomination. Evangelism operates at all levels. In defining the evangelism that decolonizes the soul, we have decided to start by stating what we know is *not evangelism*. The via negativa approach is expected to make clear what evangelism really is by pointing out what it is not. Then we will give a positive definition.

A. Evangelism is not just:
1. ... a magnificent church building (big or small), beautiful church fellowship halls, good fellowship (cliques), a population of devout church members who don't miss Sunday worship services, a gorgeous organ with a talented organist, church choir, a youth group and junior Sunday school with well educated pastors and directors. They are all very good elements to have but they do not constitute the sort of evangelism that decolonizes the soul. Good church maintenance and keeping a congregation of saints together could be like the Dead Sea which has the physical features of a sea, but neither produces nor sustains life.
2. ... numbers. Receiving members from other denominations because they cannot find their own in the vicinity, or by transfer from one's own denomination, is not evangelism. Numbers obtained this way do not signify increase to the Body of Christian believers. It is only a game of "robbing Peter to pay Paul."-- just a concert of egos. Some pastors have actually quarrelled over this. It is well known that many people transfer for reasons other than seeking Christ. A list of such reason is open-ended.
3. ... social activity devoid of spiritual vitality such as pot lucks, fundraisers, sponsored walks, boot sales, social evenings. Evangelism does not exist where the Holy Spirit is not involved.

B. As a matter of fact, we should be aware of what hinders evangelistic efforts:
1. Lack of personal knowledge of Jesus of faith in one's own life does not yield spiritual vitality no matter how many church activities the member is involved in at the church. One can not only introduce the Saviour to

others if one has not experienced the presence of the living Lord.

2. Lack of faith in Jesus Christ as the Saviour or doubts of who the Lord is.

3. Out right disobedience to the gospel "to go make disciples", (Matt. 28:19) is a very serious and deadly enemy of the spirit of evangelism. In other words, to not even make an effort to win others to Christ can be the worst foe of evangelism.

4. Spiritual "coldness" on the part of Christians robs evangelism of its natural zest and zeal. Lukewarm Christians send a negative message to the world.

5. Depriving lay people the opportunity to witness at the home church retards their spiritual growth and maturity -- hence no evangelism.

6. Finally, a pastor who is not interested nor believes in evangelising "locks up the congregation's doors to its own resurrection or growth."

C. **Regarding the discussion on what hurts church growth, we are in agreement with Peace who argues that evangelism is often distorted by three phenomena:**
   1. when it is **institutionalized** as what has happened in several mainline denominations with the basic aim of church extension in the name of recruitment (A.1.ii above);

   2. when it is **secularized** by some radical theologians who tend to equate evangelism, (however they define it,) with politics and social action in the name of "social gospel (see A.1.iii above): and

   3. when it is **"atomized'** by some conservative evangelists, in the name of "decision". Evangelism should not be reduced to just an isolated, individualistic religious experience!

II. DEFINING EVANGELISM THAT DECOLONIZES THE SOUL

The gospel of Jesus Christ decolonizes persons, families, churches, communities and the world -- setting Gods' children free to be who God intended for them to be. Evangelism that decolonizes the soul serves to rescue the soul from spiritual death, restore and nourish it unto eternal life through Christ. Jesus said: " so if the Son sets you free, you will be free indeed." [John 8:36]. St Paul also said "...if a person is in Christ Jesus, he is a new creation," [2 Corinthians 5:17].

Effective evangelism is the decolonization of persons who have been enslaved, spiritually colonized, defiled and deluded by the Devil or other forces of evil including *mweya yemadzinza* [inherited evil spirits and demons]. As former Director of Evangelism, what I have observed others doing and what I believe the Holy Spirit has led me to implement can be summed up as *decolonizing the soul; decolonizing life; bringing forth new life in Christ, setting at liberty thereby ridding the soul of various spiritual forms of bondage.* This is evangelism! *I am persuaded to define evangelism that decolonizes as, "Implementing God's supreme will to reach out to all His creation"*

Furthermore, it is a work of God's Grace and Glory performed by God's obedient Christians. To introduce Jesus to non-Christians where they may be, both in the church and in the secular world is, in fact, fulfilling our Christian responsibility. Yes, there are church members who do not know Christ. As Dr. George Barna's research showed in America "...half of all adults who attended protestant churches on a typical Sunday morning are not Christians" (*Evangelism That Works* 1995,38). Only the truly evangelised, who have a deep and sincere commitment to the redemptive Saviour have the desire, power and credibility, in partnership with the Holy Spirit who decolonizes persons can claim to **know** Jesus. Just as it is axiomatic that one blind person cannot lead another, a non-evangelised person, even if such a person is a nominal Christian, cannot lead another to the living Lord.

Evangelism that decolonizes the soul sets the converts free to proclaim the Kingdom like John the Baptist did when he cried: "Repent for the Kingdom of heaven is near" (Matt. 3:2). It steadily follows Jesus' footsteps who also preached the same message (Matt. 4:17, 10:7). A decolonizing evangelism compels followers of Jesus to meet the people at the point of their spiritual need, or depravity and introduces Jesus who decolonizes persons. Spiritually decolonized, the convert is ready to accept and experience the new rule -- the rule of love, forgiveness, peace, righteousness, joy and eternal life. The decolonized are those ready to receive the kingdom thereby enabling them to observe God's commandment: "...to love your neighbour as yourself" (Matt. 22:39), and " to do unto others what you would have them do to you" (Matt. 7:12). For the decolonized souls, only Christ is their Ruler, the rock of their salvation. All others are "sinking sand" as the hymn goes. I believe that Jesus considers Himself one ushering all creation in God's Kingdom when He announced that the Kingdom of God was present and operative among his audience. Certainly Jesus Himself was conscious of being in the world in order to transform the world, rather than being conformed to it. Only the faithful and obedient disciples are willing to assume the responsibility to spread the gospel -- only those who rightfully call themselves Christians. Yes, preaching the good news that decolonises the soul is a duty and obligation. This is why Jesus commands us to *"go!"*

I believe that inspired, spirited and Holy Spirit-guided evangelism has the power to decolonize the soul. Because God does not work in vain, evangelism will bear fruit at the set time. And now is the time because the harvest is ripe!

At a set time, Jesus dramatically faced Zaccheaus the notorious tax collector and not only did He order him to climb down but also got him to repent; "Look Lord! Here and now I give half of my possessions to the poor, and if I cheated anybody out of anything, I will pay back four times the amount." (Luke 19:8). From that time on Zacchaeus' life was transformed. He was no longer colonized with sin and greed because the Son set him free indeed. Evangelism that decolonizes the soul searches for the lost, the "Zacchaeuses" of our time and world today. Effective evangelism happens at the first instance when the Holy Spirit initially leads the obedient witness to proclaim the good news to "whomever!" Evangelism that decolonizes the soul is one more means God uses to pour His unconditional love upon His children who are in spiritual darkness. Remember, "God so loved the world that He gave His only begotten Son...." (John 3:16). Accepting Christ is what it takes to decolonize persons from sin and other forms of spiritual imprisonment. When a convert accepts Christ in his or her heart, evil has no room. One is set free indeed from the chains of evil.

For people whose minds are saturated with scepticism due to pride, abused scientific knowledge and negative energy toward Christ and the Church, as Saul of Tarsus was on the road to Damascus, and ended up preaching, (Acts 9:1-20). One hopes that such sceptics and atheists will one day not only meet the Lord but also commit themselves to serving Him. Obedience plays a major role though. Some one must preach to them first. Individuals and even a community must experience " the road to Damascus" where Christ and the Holy Spirit convict them. The Holy Spirit and sin do not co-exist.

Decolonizing a person is saving the individual from the forces of evil out there. If we do not evangelise, "In the name of Jesus," and bring the lost into the house of the Lord, the Devil, who is hard at work tempting the people of God will make an easy kill. Peter says: "your enemy, the devil prowls around like a roaring lion looking for someone to devour" (1 Pet. 5:8). Christians must obey the divine imperative to "go and teach and baptize" (Mathew 28:19-20). What is holding us back?

Thus far, it is evident that my definition of evangelism is in the company of other advocates of true evangelism. For instance we cannot agree more with Dr. Alan Walker when he says (apparently filled with and moved by the spirit of the urgency of soul saving): "Evangelism is God's word for this hour" (Walker, 1980,13) and "the motive, the passion for Evangelism comes right out of the heart of God. It must be the natural business of the Christian and the normal supreme concern of the church" (Ibid).

Regarding what evangelism is, Richard Stol Armstrong also makes a contribution to this definition in these words: "By evangelism I mean reaching out to others in Christian love, identifying with them, caring for them, listening to them, and sharing one's faith with them in such a way that they freely response and commit themselves to trust, love and obey God as disciples of Jesus and a member of His servant community, the Church" (Armstrong, 1979,53). In addition, "...evangelism is not all option. It is an imperative, and we had better be about the task" (Ibid). We agree with the thinking that one does not have to be a specially gifted evangelist to win people for Christ. What is needed is to be obedient and not just willing.

Evangelism that decolonizes makes a person a new creation. George Hunter III also makes this important point. So, we may need to heed Hunter who says: "...whatever else one might mean by evangelism, one must necessarily mean the making of new Christian disciples" (Hunter III, 1987, 21).

The process of decolonizing the soul involves the Holy Spirit who converts persons to Christ by removing the individual's spiritual burden. Incidentally, spiritual burdens are no respector of one's physical stature or social status. Some great Christians and Christian leaders were converted in different ways and various circumstances. For example Saul had to fall down from his horse and was blinded; some were imprisoned before they were converted, some became ill -- then were whisked back to health at death's door; others fell off a huge business empire and became homeless first. I could put several names and detailed stories to each one of these examples including the John Newton story which led him to compose that famous hymn "Amazing Grace" -- (See Chapter 6 for details) but space does not allow. Each one of the above had a burden uplifted in dramatic circumstances -- this is the decolonization of the soul -- not of the physical burden, but the weight on your soul -- sin, guilt.

In addition to the foregoing range of definitions, Peter De Jong put it this way: "Evangelism is participating in God's redemptive activity concerning the whole creation. It is the effort to bring men to a life of gratitude to God, the maker and redeemer of the universe" (De Jong, 1962, 630). We agree with Jong's views in part because, since evangelism is "bringing a person to Christ," the process inevitably must involve God in the form of the Holy Spirit. Evangelism is decolonizing when Christ speaks to the individual through His love, grace and assurance. "Peace be with you! As the father sent me I am sending you" (John 20:21). He sends us to introduce His love and liberating grace to other persons who are colonized by Satan. Decolonizing such persons occurs when the individual accepts Christ in one's heart and converts or repents. My Dear Reader, trust me, it works. Let us *go do it!*

Interesting enough, we are not sent to the world in general, rather there are specific persons out there to evangelise: the individual, a family, a businessman or a businesswoman, a student, a chief, a motherless child, a doctor, a girl, a patient, a professor, a government official, a head of state, a dictator, a traditional healer, the rich, the poor and the list goes on. The point is that God who cares for each one of them wants them saved. So those who know Christ are sent to evangelise. Woe unto them if they should resist being sent.

In my opinion, those who believe that they do not need Christ are in a special category of potential converts. The challenge of the evangelist is to "bring such people to the awareness" that they are in fact lost without Christ who gives life. Unless genuine Christians witness this category, they are denied salvation. Fortunately, the Holy Spirit will visit them at a set time not known to any human being.

I agree with George Morris' statement that the world thinks it knows what it wants but does not know what it needs (Morris, 1980, 82). The evidence that the world needs Christ lies in it's very fallacious belief that it doesn't need Him while they are hurting. They are like a diabetic who may be pricked by a nail but does not sense it; or an epileptic victim who, under seizures, may be thrown into fire and burn without sensing it since the senses are numb. So, evangelism that decolonizes the person begins to take effect when the heart becomes receptive to the Word and the person becomes aware of the need to be free -- to be redeemed from bondage. At the risk of sounding paternalistic, at times I believe that some people need to be assisted to discover who they are and what they need in order to live a purposeful life. Our responsibility as Christians involves presenting Christ to those in darkness in such a way that they awaken to the reality of needing a saviour and the certainty of spiritual revitalization. Some people do not know who they are.

When I was a college freshman in 1959, for my Christmas break I was the guest of the late Bishop and Mrs Alton of Wisconsin. A newspaper reporter keenly interviewed this foreign student attending Missouri School of Religion in Columbia, Missouri. The next day I was shocked to read the article in the local paper depicting me as "…. a shy, soft-spoken gentleman." Certainly this description did not fit me, "Shy?" Certainly not me; "Soft-spoken?" Again not me! However my wife, Maggie, has since reminded me repeatedly that whenever I preach, I must speak a little louder, please. Yes, some people need to be made aware who they are. Some people need to be reminded it is time to give up that torn and tattered jacket, some need to be told to trade-in that troublesome old car, some need to be urged to upgrade their appearance -- get a make over; and similarly, other people have to be told that they need Christ. There are some people wondering why, despite all their material success, they do not feel a sense of satisfaction. Why? Why are they not happy when they have everything material that one ever needs in order to be happy? There is one thing needful.

Jesus Christ is the Missing Link

We need to share the gospel message with them: a person "does not live by bread alone, but on every word that comes from the mouth of God" (Matt. 4:4). Ideally, a human being is a religious, physical, social, psychological and spiritual being. Jesus also said: "seek first the Kingdom of God and His righteousness, and all other things will be added to them" (Matt. 6:33). The gospel invites every human being under the sun to repent (Matt. 4:7) and follow Jesus.

I am convinced that the real business of the Church is to serve as God's instrument and means of salvation. To do that, it must be spirit-filled and spirit-led. When the maintenance church (we described earlier in this chapter) begins to have a mission statement set up, decent budget for outreach, the pastor starts preaching evangelistic sermons, and educating the members as well as training them to reach out to the unchurched, and actually praying for the winning of the unchurched, then it has graduated from the "Dead Sea Stage" and, in fact, it is resurrecting. When both the pastor and the congregation go out to reach out to those who are lost, then and only then can that church say: *"We are doing the work of evangelism." "We are obedient to Jesus who instructs us to make disciples." "We have become an obedient, faithful and fruitful church of Jesus Christ."* That church has become one of the soldiers of Christ in the warfare of disarming the devil and decolonizing people who have been captured by the power of darkness.

It is a frightening thought to wonder what would happen if every adult in the world were non-Christian or worse still, if everyone were as evil as the devil, and if they were filled with evil spirits, guided by the power of evil, if they never heard about the love of God, or Jesus Christ. What kind of a world would this be? My estimation is that it would be real hell on earth. Human beings would live just like animals -- with no moral standards, no sense of justice, no sense of divine purpose, and no peace!

But God in His foreknowledge gave His only begotten Son that whoever believes in Him shall not perish but have everlasting life. In addition, God's will has been revealed to humanity through God-become-man (Incarnation), and the challenge now is to preach God's love and God's Christ so that the world may repent, and acknowledge the Saviour, Jesus Christ. To accomplish this, what is needed -- what will do the job effectively is an evangelism that decolonizes all souls. Yes, we need to reclaim all the souls from power of darkness to Light, which is the Life.

Now, may the Grace of our Lord Jesus, the Love of God the Father, and the fellowship of the Holy Spirit bless you all...Amen.

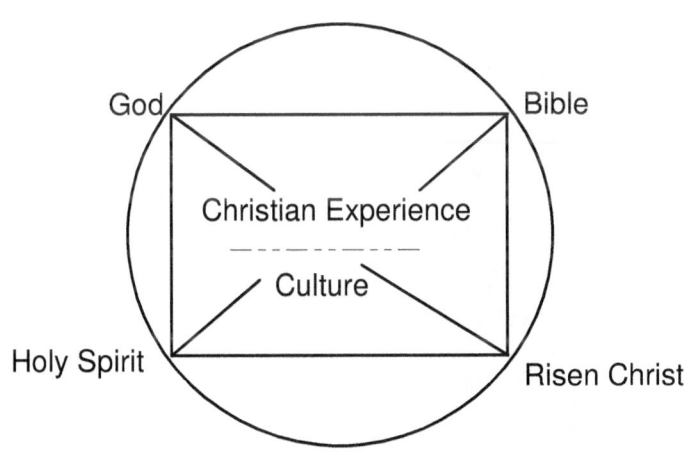

The EDS Model

Five
INSTRUMENTS AND MEANS OF EVANGELISM

> *In the Sermon on the Mount, Jesus said, "Which of you, if his son asks for bread, will give him a stone? Or if he asks for fish will give him a snake? If you then, though you are evil know how to give good gifts to your children, how much more will your father in heaven give good gifts to those who ask Him?" (Matt. 7:9-11).*

Evangelism is meaningful when it gives the people what they need, rather than what they want. Since Jesus came so that "they may have life and have it abundantly," it is only reasonable to preach Jesus so that all may live the abundant life, which Christ promises. But, what means and instruments should evangelism employ? In this chapter we discuss what we consider the major means of evangelising, namely prayer and preaching. In his struggle in Gethsemane the night before His crucifixion, Jesus said to His disciples, "Watch and pray..." (Matt. 26:41). Paul, writing to the Thessalonians said, "Pray without ceasing" (1 Thess. 5:17). Numerous Scriptures point to the importance of what the soul needs, rather than some superfluous desire of the heart. In my experience, I have come to the conclusion that there is wonder-working power in prayer.

I. THE POWER OF PRAYER

The entire village and district of Mutoko was broken hearted, sad and gloomy because a loved member of the royal family, the chief of the area, was very sick. He was actually at the point of dying. Strangely enough, one morning he whispered to his son in a voice so faint it was hard to understand. His message was that he had a dream in which the *Vabvuwi*[8] were praying for him, *Vabvuwi* are known to pray for healing, demon exorcism, bringing persons to Christ and the like. Being one of the *Vabvuwi* himself, the chief's son took the dream seriously; he urgently informed the leader of the local *Vabvuwi* what his father had said. Furthermore, he implored them to grant his father what might well have been a dying wish. They agreed to visit the patient the following morning, if he was still living.

To prepare themselves spiritually, they would meet at a certain place -- in the bush -- at four o'clock in the morning and do what amounted to ritual

---

[8] "Fishermene" - The official name is *Mubvuwi we United Methodist Church* (MUMC), denoting United Methodist Church men.

cleansing. After exchanging greetings, the leader proposed that each of them, starting with himself, must confess their sins publicly, right there and then, before they began the intercessory prayer (James 5:16). The leader said anyone who did not want to do so could feel free to excuse himself quietly while everyone's eyes were closed, as they knelt singing a hymn. Sure enough a few of the men left. Those who remained took turns to pray. They were on their knees until about noon.

When they felt they were spiritually ready, they strolled toward the chief's homestead, singing one of the well-known healing hymns: *"Murapi aripano, chiremba wekudenga. Wauya pasi pano korapa mwoyo yese. ..."* (The heavenly physician is here to heal every sin-sick soul).

Then came the miracle; as they approached the chief's homestead, to their amazement, they found him walking aided by his walking stick, something he was no longer able to do. He was actually inspecting his homestead to see what had changed while confined to his bed. Greeted with this amazing sight, a miracle, they started singing at the top of their voices joyously. There was jubilant dancing and praising God with grateful hearts. In the name of Jesus of Nazareth the chief had been healed without any medication or physical contact! They learned that he had started feeling better in the early hours of that morning, the very time, the *Vabvuwi* were praying in the bush.

One cannot over emphasize the fact that faith healing is never to be relegated to "old fashioned religion." For the faithful, God is still performing miracles, including intercessory healing in the name of Jesus. Prayer is absolutely necessary for evangelism that decolonizes the soul, and miracles make evangelism efficacious. Miracles are one way among many that God shows us that when we seek His presence and help, He does respond, though in His own time. One need not over emphasize that the life of faith is inseparable from prayerful life. Our Lord Jesus had a track record of prayer life and miracles.

A. Jesus at Prayer

It blesses and encourages Christians to know that Jesus took prayer seriously even though He was "...very God and very man"[9]. He humbled Himself and was dependent on God. For Jesus, prayer was an important instrument with which to keep tuned-in to His Father. The result was that His ministry was extremely effective, and He overcame "the prince of darkness," through prayer. It is no wonder, we often find him praying in various other situations. Jesus preferred to pray alone as the gospel tells us: "Very early in the morning while it was dark

---

[9] Article II: Doctrinal Standards and General Rules, United Methodist Church, page 59. "The Son, who is the Word of the Father, the very and eternal God, of one substance with the Father, took man's nature in the womb of the blessed Virgin; so that two whole and perfect natures. that is to say, the Godhead and Manhood, were joined together in one person, never to be divided; whereof is one Christ, very God and very Man, who truly suffered. was crucified. dead, and buried, to reconcile his Father to us, and to be sacrifice, not only for original guilt, but also for actual sins of men.

Jesus got up, left the house and went off to a solitary place, where He prayed" (Mark 1:35, Luke 4:42). When He fed the 5000 people, He first offered a thanksgiving prayer (John 6:11). He prayed for all believers (John 17:20-26) and for His disciples (John 17:6-19). However Jesus spoke sharply and strongly against those who would pray as a way of showing off like Pharisees did because prayer is serious business. "Such men will be punished most severely" (Mark 12:40). Only God can tell the sincere and earnest prayers of a person, and He knows the motives. Prayer is power when it is offered from the bottom of the heart, and is consistent with God's will or God's agenda.

Jesus' prayerful life must have touched, moved and led the disciples to ask, "Lord, teach us to pray." Not only did Jesus teach them to pray, He set an example in Gethsemane -- the last night when He was facing the cup. As the Son of God, Jesus asked His father's will and not His own to be done. Needless to say, prayer serves various purposes including giving us courage and hope as well as preparing us to deal with whatever situation might befall us. Prayer is a matter of grave concern. Those who pray must do so in truth and by faith. Jesus' Gethsemane experience must have been a painful, serious internal struggle. He told His disciples openly: "My soul is overwhelmed with sorrow to the point of death" (Matt. 26:38). With His face to the ground, be prayed, "My father, if it is possible may this cup be taken from me. Yet not as I will" (Matt. 26:39). Teaching by example, Jesus tells us to face important and crucial decisions on our knees in prayer because *a prayer of faith moves God.* When we pray, we ought to bow our hearts before Him...and yet, how many crucial decisions do we make without involving God? How many?

Jesus ordered His disciples through the Holy Spirit and He admonishes us today to "watch and pray, so that you will not enter into temptations" (Matt. 26:41). We ought to watch and pray so that we are strong disciples and workers of Jesus Christ. Constant contact with God through prayer is spiritually rejuvenating, and those who are thus energized are best able to evangelise effectively. One can never overstate what Jesus has done for all humanity, for which we must be grateful. Even as He was hanging on the cross Jesus prayed for His enemies: "Father, forgive them, for they do not know what they are doing" (Luke 23:34).

B. The Early Church at Prayer

The early church took prayer as an instrument and means of evangelising. They were keen, enthusiastic, obedient and devout disciples who had learned about the secret of prayer from their rabbi, Jesus and from the Day of Pentecost in the upper room. Miraculous events had taught them that prayer must be treated as a priority because it invokes power -- Holy Ghost Power. For example in Acts 4:1 we read that the Jews wanted to try and punish or even kill Peter and John as they had murdered James, because the former had healed the lame man at the gate of the temple called Beautiful (Acts 4:23). "After they prayed, the place where they were meeting was shaken, and they were all filled with the Holy Spirit and spoke the word of God boldly (Acts 4:31). They got fuelled up to go on witnessing about Jesus in spite of danger posed by their persecutor. In Acts 12, we also read Peter's suffering, arrest and imprisonment. He was to be tried and executed, but the Church, meeting in the house of John Mark's mother, (Acts 12:3) prayed for him apparently *pungwe (*the whole night). Peter was miraculously released from jail. Paul and Silas were also jailed. But while in jail, they decided to pray, praising God through song. According to this account, the handcuffs broke and the door of the jail opened. As if that was not enough, the jailer ended up being baptized along with his entire household (Acts 16:22-31). Again, prayer is key to various situations. For instance, when the early church wanted to choose outstanding deacons, they prayed for divine guidance (Acts 6:6). The New Testament is full of examples of how prayer brought about solutions to difficult situations.

C. Today's Church at Prayer

If we should be effective disciples in evangelising the world we had better pray. Numerous revival meetings are held throughout the Christian world. While some are indeed revivals with fruitful results, my suspicion is that others are definitely not because of lack of thorough preparation, i.e. lack of prayer for the Holy Spirit to take over. As a result, nothing really happens. They are simply gatherings of religious people, nothing more. I contend that revival meetings that lack prayers of faith will yield no converts, no revived souls, and no decolonized persons. Differently put, the element of renewal is missing. The spiritual refilling that is the prerequisite for "revival" is non-existent. True revival meetings must assume the work of the Holy Spirit. True revivals are productive in terms of converts, born again persons, refilled souls, healing and other manifestations of the presence of the Holy Spirit. Very often one hears testimonies of changed lives and renewed commitments. All this comes through prayer – "praying without ceasing."

How should we prepare for genuine, spiritual, fruitful revivals? When such meetings are planned, disciples of Jesus must spend earnest quality time and long devoted time praying for God's reviving spirit to descend upon the worshippers. Evangelists engage in prayer for several weeks, months or even longer to invoke the Holy Spirit. The would-be evangelist must engage in earnest prayer for the Holy Spirit to ignite their souls, which in turn revives other worshippers. Generally when we pray for the Holy Spirit like the Pentecost of Jerusalem and the Holy Spirit of 1918 at Old Mutare, we must have extraordinary faith, be obedient, patient and receptive. Bishop Nhiwatiwa said; "The spirit of 1918 did not happen in a vacuum. There were prayers asking God to shower the people with the power of the Holy Spirit (*Humble Beginnings* p.74).

A story was told of Charles Haddon Spurgeon of Metropolitan Tabernacle in London who was a fiery preacher. Whenever they organized a revival, the community was filled with the Holy Spirit and the participants experienced the truly reviving spirit. Out of curiosity, a group of five students from a nearby seminary decided to visit Pastor Spurgeon in order to find out what was the secret of his successful revivals. Rather than give them an academic explanation, the pastor took them to a prayer-hall with 700 serious Christians who were on their knees praying for the services before the pastor even got to the pulpit. "There!" He said. "There is the secret." Come to think of it, it was actually a public secret.

Since prayer is such a public secret, what does one pray for? One should always pray for the immediate needs and then extend the circle to less pressing needs.

1. **Pray for a lost family member:**

    In Chapter One I stated that our parents had nine children. Although they taught everyone Christian life style, one of the boys turned his back on it all in spite of the conducive family atmosphere. He went his own way -- in plain and simple Christian-terms, he was lost. In the context of our family it is fair to describe him as the *white sheep* of the family, the odd one. Needless to say, our parents were both disappointed that this son decided not to be a practicing Christian in spite of his infant baptism and the great name they gave him: John Wesley. Fortunately, they believed in the power of prayer. Our mother went deep into intense prayer of faith that someday God would intervene and convict this handsome young man. In our teens and early adult lives, every night she would pray in tears, crying to beseech God to save her son, John Wesley Kufahakutizwi, from his spiritual wilderness and darkness.

    Our father lived over eighty-two years. When he died his son had not accepted Christ, yet up to the end, he still had the faith and hope that one day God would bring him back into the fold. I praise the Lord that my mother *did* live to see her prayers answered. In his late forties, John Wesley accepted Christ as his personal saviour. Not only did he become a Christian, but also a preacher in the United Methodist Church.

    Dear Reader, if you believe in Prayer and you have loved ones and friends who are lost, pray for them because there is a wonder working power in the name of Jesus! This reminds me of my childhood Christian chorus. We used to sing: "Why worry, when you can pray. Trust in Jesus, He will be your guide..." Unfortunately these days it seems as though Christians have twisted the lyrics to say: "Why pray when you can worry, trust in science, it will be your guide?" I am convinced that there is a lot to pray for.

2. **Pray for the needy:**

    Pray for the needy -- loved ones, friends, schoolmates, the sick and the poor. Many people are in great need out there. For instance, some years ago there was a couple from Congo, now the Democratic Republic of Congo, (D.R.C.), who came to Old Mutare Mission to study. They had gone for fifteen years without a child yet they wanted very badly to have one. Unfortunately, they could not. All the medical know-how had failed. One day, the Methodist women, inspired by the Holy Spirit, decided to pray for her that she might conceive. After singing moving hymns, they then laid their hymnals and Bibles on her body and took turns to pray for her. After nine months she had a baby boy whom the parents named Samuel, as did Hannah of the Old Testament. (1 Sam. 1-2). The couple went back to D.R.C with their son, Samuel, who became a medical doctor and is still practicing at the time of writing. For those who witnessed this miracle, they know that the power of prayer is so efficacious that no one needs to convince them.

Unfortunately, not all of us are so privileged, and not many of us honestly, deeply and truly believe in regular prayer. *Blessed are those who believe in the power of prayer, and they take prayer seriously.*

3. **Pray for Holiness:**

After his involvement in Uriah's death, and the adulterous affair with Bathsheeba, Uriah's wife, King David of Israel prayed for himself: "Have mercy on me, O God...blot out my transgression. Wash away all my iniquity and cleanse me from my sin" (Psalm 51:1-2). The Bible clearly tells us God's position regarding sin. God says, "Oh come, let us reason together even if your sin is as red as scarlet, ..." The problem today, in some parts of the globe, there are those who believe that there is nothing to confess while they live in sin. The Bible also reminds us that we have all fallen short of the glory of God. We sin, but God through Jesus has made a provision for our forgiveness, if we acknowledge the Saviour. Since it is God who justifies and sanctifies us, all we need to do is pray. Only God is the source of Holiness, and only He sanctifies us. God commands us to "be perfect" (Matt. 5:48).

4. **Pray for your enemies**:

Although it is not the easiest thing to do, the Bible tells us to pray, not only for our loved ones but for our enemies as well. Since prayer serves to put us in tune with God, it is reasonable for one to pray for whatever circumstances one may find oneself in. Psalm 23 is a good example of one who believed in the Lord so much that he brings in "God even in the midst of his enemies," believing that the Lord will protect him at all times. "He prepares a table for me in the presence of my enemies" (Psalm 23). Also in the Old Testament, David goes to battle to fight Goliath, "in the name of the Lord." Therefore, if the Lord helps us in our struggles against our enemies, we do well to pray for them so that, with God's blessing, they may become our friends. Certainly, so they may not pose the threat that makes them our enemies. Praying for our enemies is an act of making peace, which is what the gospel teaches: "Blessed are the peacemakers, for they shall be called the children of God (Matt. 5:9), pray-pray-pray. Pray in private, and God who sees in private will reward you publicly (Matt. 5:6-7).

In Zimbabwean United Methodist Church circles, people talk a lot about "*paka,*" a place where an individual or a group goes to pray -- usually in the bush, mountains or some such place.[10] We pray to praise God, to thank Him and to seek His will; praying for our enemies makes this world a better place. Wouldn't this world be an ideal community if we all loved each other? One of the marks of the people I regard as Christian giants is their Christ-like lifestyle. Christ forgave all His enemies even as He was hanging on the ignominious cross on Mt. Calvary.

5. **God answers all prayers:**

Christian spiritual giants believe that God answers all prayers according to His will and foreknowledge. I think it is spiritual immaturity to expect God to always grant us what we ask for because, most of the time, we do not even know what we really need in order to live a meaningful life. So, when God says "No" to what we ask Him, that answer is as good as "Yes". God loves us and looks after our welfare even before we become aware of the circumstances surrounding us. God's "No" does not negate His love and caring for us, just as we say "No" to a child we love very much when it cries for a razor blade or sharp knife; no matter how much they plead with us, because we know they will hurt themselves, we say "No". We have known people whom God blessed with wealth; those very riches then changed their character into unpleasant, mean people. My theory is that this happens because God does not micromanage our lives. We have free will. It is not always the case, but there are numerous examples of people I know personally who ruined their lives either because they had become more educated (rather mis-educated), wealthier, or they ascended to the position of power and comfort. Let me single out one example.

There was a time when it was easier to seek tertiary education abroad than in Zimbabwe. My cousin, who had a beautiful wife and kids, did not have a college degree. Both husband and wife always prayed for an opportunity to go overseas for further education. After I worked hard to send him overseas for higher education, he indeed got a degree but he also became a bigamist, an alcoholic and just downright a useless schooled man who would neither provide for his family nor take any responsibility for the community that raised him. The man has since died -- and he died a shameful death -- the family is still in disarray and in a spiritual wilderness. God might as well have said, "No" to his wish for a college degree.

Again, as I said earlier, things do not have to be that way; but we say this to make the point that it is much better to pray for God's will for us than just pray for whatever we think will make our lives better; because, as the author of Ecclesiastes correctly observed and stated, "all is vanity if God is left out" (Ecclesiastes 5:1f). But God does not always say "No". Sometimes God says "wait" for the *kairos* moment.

---

[10] Remember Elijah in the cave, Peter on the rooftop in Jopah and Jesus in the garden of Gesthemane. See Mark 1:35, Luke 4:42. Probably the word originated from the term 'prayer *park.*'

6. **The right moment in time:**
To some prayers, God's answer is "wait". Many people stop praying when they don't get what they requested from God. The general thinking and expectations by most people is that for a prayer to be considered answered, it should always be "Yes" and the answer must come promptly. They want instant gratification. If they don't get it then they stop praying. Is this not similar to throwing a tantrum? Yet when we pray we should trust God's foreknowledge. God's answer may be "Wait" a while for the right time for what you are praying for. Regarding prayer, in the parable of the persistent widow, Jesus urges us to be persistent (Luke 18:1-8). Some mature Christians have experienced that God answers a lot of prayers but He takes His time. Effective evangelism will always be productive even if we do not count converts right away. The parable of The Sower teaches us that all we must do is broadcast the "word" (seed), and let each heart respond. As we wait for the maize seed to ferment and germinate, so should we wait for the word to "take hold" and eventually show results.

II. THE POWER OF THE SERMON

Preaching is another powerful instrument and means of evangelism that decolonizes the soul. The power of speech is never to be underestimated. Take a baby who does not yet know how to speak. But it screams and effectively gets what it needs by that method of communicating. If it is hungry, thirsty, uncomfortable (wet clothes, sleepy, sick), it simply cries loudly and the whole family will have to pay attention to it. The mother is moved to action by love, kindness and a sense of responsibility.

Speech appeals to people's emotions, especially when it is intended to accomplish some goal. A sermon is a form of speech. What we do with it can move persons to respond in one way or another. If it is done properly, a sermon will move the hearer to respond, verbally or by action. Some sermons have caused the audience to sob, to be sad, to be angry, or driven them to positive action.

There is power in the Holy Spirit inspired sermon. Jesus left us the sermon on the mountain. If most of the Bible would be lost and we remained with just the sermon on the mountain, we still would have sufficient gospel to go by as Christians, I believe. For example if everybody, Christian and non-Christian, lived by Matthew 7:12, "So in everything, do to others what you would have them do to you," there would be peace in one's heart, in homes, communities, nations and the world. Preaching God's word has a way to bring peace and reconciliation, but preaching our own wisdom may not be as efficacious. In conclusion, one can never overstate the importance of a spirit-filled sermon, inspired by God to be delivered to His people. Chapter 7 talks more about the virtues of an evangelistic sermon.

III. THE POWER OF LIVING PERSONAL TESTIMONIES

Umbowo[11], living personal testimonies, like Christian experience which we have discussed in Chapter Three is one of the instruments and means of evangelism that decolonizes persons. In other words, your Christian experiences are manifested as testimonies which have the effect of evangelising others.

Most of what we read in the Bible is personal *umbowo* of people who experienced God's grace and redeeming agape. In the Old Testament, Exodus, for instance, is *umbowo* of how the nation of Israel experienced God's intervening grace and deliverance from captivity. In the New Testament, Acts is full of apostles' *umbowo*. In fact, the New Testament is replete with individuals' *umbowo*. Some use their umbowo to defend themselves when attacked on account of their faith. The ultimate *umbowo*, is that of Mary Magdalene, who declared, "I have seen the Lord. He is risen," (John 20:18). We should encourage *umbowo*.

But what is a *umbowo*/testimony anyway? It is simply acknowledging what God or His Son Jesus or the Holy Spirit has done in one's life. A *umbowo* not shared is a sermon not preached! *Umbowo* can be a vehicle through which what God has done, or is doing in one's life is conveyed. People who want to stand before the church and tell others what God has done for them should be encouraged to share their *umbowo,* especially of conversion, repentance, forgiveness, the power of the Holy Spirit, and so forth. Genuine *umbowo* are indeed some of the most powerful means of drawing others to Christ and encouraging them to trust Jesus, the Saviour. *Umbowo* help to dispel doubt. They encourage others to keep praying because they affirm that God is still answering prayers, even if your own prayer is on hold -- in kairos.

I will never forget the time I was in seminary at Old Mutare Mission. We used to have joint services with people of Penhalonga, a nearby mining community. There was a tiny woman with hardly any education. Her appearance and stature gave no clue to the power she wielded when she spoke. Whenever she stood up to speak, most of the time men and women would end up in tears -- moved by her personal *umbowo*; she too would often shed tears. She had been powerfully and dramatically converted by the power of Jesus Christ.

Indeed personal *umbowo* can be a blessing as we see in the following example. The gift of God came to Zimbabwe through the dramatic conversion of a man to whom I will repeatedly return in this book -- Rev. Conrad Chigumira -- a Holy Spirit filled and miracle-working preacher. His sermons were powerful because they were dominated by powerful personal *umbowo*. Converts who share how they accepted Christ are a living example of how God works by grace to redeem sinners.

Yes, Jesus can speak today and what He says is our *umbowo* to share. One day, before I retired, I was asked to preach at the Annual Convention of the United Methodist Women in Zimbabwe, which was held at a camp site by the

---

[11] Both singular and plural.

river near Nyadire Mission Centre. There were about 8000 worshippers, mostly RRW members. Among the few men present was one of the most dignified headmasters of our schools, Josephat Banda who responded to my sermon in a special manner. My message was *"God speaks to people today,"* based on Hebrews 1:1-3. During the altar call I ordered that no one should sing or pray out loud, which is the norm in Zimbabwe. On this occasion, I asked each person present to be quiet -- listening to God. After the listening period, I asked if there were some people who had heard God speaking to them. Amongst them, Josephat Banda, a headmaster, stood up and testified, "God told me to quit teaching and go to theological school to become a preacher." The least we could do was pray for him and bless him. He did that. Everybody who knows him will agree he is one of our most committed ministers. To date he has served for over twenty years. As I am writing this book, he has just completed another six years as District Superintendent.

In sum *umbowo* can be the embodiment of God's voice, grace or love. Therefore, I urge all Christians not to be so modest that they choose not to share their *umbowo*. This also applies to new converts. In the next chapter we will return to this topic to discuss the importance to new converts of *umbowo* as a way of cementing faith.

IV. POWER IN MUSIC!

Martin Luther, the great reformer once said, "...music is a gift of God. It will drive the devil out, and make men, (sic) forget all wrath." It is a known fact that music touches the heart. Even people who cannot sing can be touched and moved by good, well presented, and well orchestrated singing. It has also been said that music is the language of the soul. Music therefore is another instrument and means to evangelism that decolonizes souls. Music wields the same power as speech or sermon. It can move persons to say or do one thing or the other. Look at what it did to King Saul of Israel. The Bible says, "Whenever the spirit that tormented the soul came upon him," David who had been hired as an accomplished musician, "... would take up his harp and play. Then relief would come to Saul; he would feel better; and the evil spirit would leave him," (I Sam. 16:23). In this incident music was used to bring peace and tranquillity to the troubled soul of the king. Music literally decolonized Saul's soul.

Christians have been enriched individually and collectively by the Psalms of David which are a blessing to all who read them because they are deep human emotions which are expressed in song. Many have been converted, encouraged or comforted through the message conveyed in the Psalms.

The power of words in music created a deadly jealous attitude in Saul's spirit. For example, women praised David who had killed Goliath, the notoriously dangerous Philistine warrior, and despised Saul. "As they danced, they sang, "Saul has slain thousands, and David his tens of thousands," (1 Sam. 18:7). Apart from arousing one's emotions music has a cognitive effect as well.

It conveys a message and even moves souls to repentance. At our revival camp meetings in Zimbabwe, hundreds of converts are ultimately moved by Christian evangelistic singing. One of my favourite stories best demonstrates the power of music.

A young man, I will pseudonym Frank, belonged to a gang whose business was robbery and even murder. He carried a big knife to strike fear in his victims or to strike them dead if they did not yield to his demands. Each night the gang would spread out across town seeking opportunities to do evil. At daybreak they would meet to share the spoils.

One night the gang members were assigned to different directions of the city, as usual. Frank, happened to pass by a church where people were having their praise and worship service. The thug had never in his life heard people sing like that! So out of curiosity, he decided to join the worshipers. He followed the melodious voices and entered the sanctuary without drawing attention to himself. He sat right by the door so he could slip out anytime he was ready to proceed on his evil mission. The miracle as well as the saving grace manifested as the longer he sat there, the more the music touched his soul. Deeper and deeper, the music penetrated until it reached a corner of his heart he did not know was there. His conscience was aroused and before long, it was time for the sermon which was based on Isaiah 1:18, "Though your sins are like scarlet, they shall be as white as snow; though they are red as crimson, they shall be like wool."

Frank remained in the church until every body had left, except the pastor. Then he strolled towards the altar to meet and ask the preacher: "Is it true that no matter what kind of sin one has committed he can be forgiven by God?"

The pastor replied, "If you are very sorry in your heart, for the sin you have committed, God will forgive. Yes."

Then Frank went on, "What if a person committed murder? Can that be forgiven?"

The pastor answered, "Yes."

"What if he killed two people?" Frank pressed.

The pastor replied, "He can be forgiven."

At that point Frank started weeping, fell at the pastor's feet and confessed, "Reverend, I killed 15 innocent people, I now hate to think of it, I am sorry."

That night a young lost soul was saved from his sins. It all started with the sweet, strong sound of music that had the power to attract his attention and lure him to salvation -- literally "to tame this savage beast." Praise be to God, through music, when the gang got back together at daybreak, Frank was not among them. Neither did he miss the gang.

The power of gospel music accompanied with evangelistic preaching fueled by prayer of great faith, will produce the desired fruit in evangelising. This is why I argue that music is an important instrument of evangelism -- evangelism that decolonizes the soul. Furthermore, the power of music runs across all cultures. England had reached "the lowest ebb" when the hymns composed by Charles Wesley, who accompanied his brother and preacher, John Wesley, helped save it through spirit-filled music and the word of God. The Africans and their cousins the African-Americans have been blessed and talented naturally with rhythm. Consequently, the world's most moving Negro spirituals are an excellent example of music that touches the soul. So why don't we make the best of it in praising and glorifying God? God must have given us that gift for a purpose. Hey! Beat that drum, child of God!

V. PLANNING EVANGELISTIC MUSIC SERVICE

As we have already illustrated above, music can be a very effective way of luring new converts to Christ. It can be just as effective at renewing spirituality as a sermon. Music and worship go hand in glove. A worship service without music is as incomplete as a day without sunshine. It is therefore important to incorporate it into every service. Music can even stand alone as an entire service.

A. Planning a music service is easy but it must begin well in advance.
1. First announce to the congregation and community a few weeks in advance that on such a date, (perhaps a month away) there will be an evangelistic music service. Your announcement must emphasize that this is an alternative method of worship -- something 'special' and out of the ordinary -- something that is not to be missed. Call for a lot of prayer for it in church and homes. Repeat the announcement weekly, as necessary. Encourage members to each invite some special guests, friends, co-worker, neighbours.

2. Appoint a talented warm spirited music leader for the day.

3. Plan with the choir to sing well-known hymns to be sung by the entire congregation with the highest degree of spiritual intensity. It is important for the congregation to be involved and not be merely an inactive audience. Hence:
    a. Ask the choir to sing soul-challenging songs, including some new pieces that the congregation has not heard before.
    b. Choose most penetrating, popular choruses for congregational singing.
    c. Beat that drum(s) and other music instruments to praise God. Yes, it adds to spiritual vitality. Use them!

I noticed when the use of drums and *hoshos* was allowed in our worship services, the spiritual vitality increased; our worship service became a moving experience, as opposed to the time we sang only our traditional hymns, standing like dead wood. A good example of how praise and worship should be conducted is found in Psalm 47:1,5,6,7.

B. Music Service Order of Worship:
Following weeks of serious prayer time for its success, on the actual day an

evangelistic music service may be organized and run like this:

1. Without too many preliminaries, let there be an opening evangelistic sermon by someone best qualified to do that. It must be very short to allow more time for singing -- a sermonette.

2. Congregational singing (choruses). Sing all the verses in order to get the full meaning of the song, thereby touching the soul.

3. Congregational hymns sung with power. Choose those that seem to touch most people -- sing a little longer than usual.

4. Ask for favourites from non-regular church attendees. Sing powerfully. This may prepare them for the closing altar call.

5. Ask the choir to sing at least two of their most powerful selections. If the song causes some members of the congregation to join in, encourage it.

6. Congregational singing -- most powerfully. Select those that lead people to truly worship, cry, be comforted, be encouraged, be joyful, and repent.

7. A final most powerful song, as people are invited to the altar.

8. Allow testimonies, if there are any. It is prudent to have planned these ahead.

9. Choose a suitable song as people pass the love and peace in the pews.

10. Benediction can be spoken or sung.

Try it. With God's help, it can not go wrong. Don't forget to have a plan for the harvest of souls that will follow[12].

---

[12] PS: At the end of the service and in the weeks following, you should canvas opinions on whether this should be an annual or bi-annual special programme. One practical way of organising this is to plan it around the time your choir is practising for choral competitions or some other music ministry outreach. The evangelistic music service can improve in stature each time it is attempted and it can produce better results each time it is performed. Variations of the programme outlined above must be tried to suit each local church's individual situation. Remember that music is a very important component of your worship services and therefore it should be given adequate attention and emphasis.

Six
EVANGELISM THAT PRODUCES DEFINITE RESULTS

Throughout the Christian tradition, it has been established that successful evangelism is characterized by obedience to the Holy Spirit. God's word commands us to "Go", and go we must.

OBEDIENCE

Jesus' command is clear and precise. Any "liberals" who don't believe in the great commission, based on Matt. 28:19, need to be reminded that being "liberals" does not mean disobedience to God's commands. In fact, I challenge any Christians who regard themselves as liberals to manifest a radical obedience such as we see in Jesus -- a Jewish radical with a track record of successful evangelism that decolonizes souls based on obedience to God.

I. PERSONAL EVANGELISM METHOD

Personal evangelism is truly the best method of spiritually decolonizing souls -- claiming lost souls from darkness to Jesus Christ, the Light of the world. Paul says "through Him (Jesus Christ) and for His namesake, we received grace and apostleship to call people from among all the gentiles to the obedience that comes from faith" (Rom. 1:5). Paul was addressing the Roman Church, which was largely Christianised through personal evangelism! As William MacDonald has said: "If we have found Christ, then let us pass on our experience to others. That was how Christianity spread in the Roman Empire, and that is how Christ will reclaim His place in the hearts of men and women today" (MacDonald, 1936,167).

There is a legend that says after Jesus returned to heaven, dignitaries of heaven surrounded Him to hear what He achieved on earth. His answer was simple: "I preached, healed, saved sinners." He was then asked: now that you have left the earth, who will save the world? He confidently answered, "I have appointed my disciples to carry on." Another question, "What if they will not do it?" Jesus paused, looked down in silence and seemingly sad he said, "If my disciples will not do what I told them to do, I have no other plan to save the world."

Yes, the heavens' expectation is that Christians will obey Jesus and spread the gospel. Trust and obedience to Jesus is the most effective evangelistic characteristic in spreading the gospel.

And what is the gospel? William J. Abraham would say, "It is the unique narrative of what God has done to maturate His kingdom in Jesus Christ of Nazareth, crucified and buried out of Jerusalem, risen from the dead, seated at the right hand of God, and now reigning eternally with the Father through the activity of the Holy Spirit in the church and in the world" (Abraham, 1996, 170). It is Christians and only Christians who are expected to spread the gospel in the world. Part of being a Christian is deciding to be obedient and to fulfil the gospel imperative. We must choose the most effective way of doing it.

After examining various types of evangelism methods, and from my personal experience, I have come to the conclusion that the most effective and successful method, which has been implemented repeatedly with best results, is *personal evangelism*. I have used it in many situations and it worked. I have observed others using it with good results because of its advantages which I will state. However it must also be noted that the one and only problem that would cause failure where this method is applied, is the pastor, of course. We shall return for the detailed look at the pastor in the final Chapter; for now let us put it to you that doubting "Thomases," faithless, simply burned out or lazy pastors are a stumbling block to personal evangelism.

This method is indeed fruitful! Thousands upon thousands of churches and various denominations that tried this method have had nothing but praises for it. They are excited with the outcome in their spiritual maturity and they thank God for their success. In fact, this often turns out to be a humbling experience. Among its advantages is it provides steady growth. Some churches have reported quadruple growth in membership in a short space of time. Another of its advantages is it is tried and tested, by Jesus, and He thanked God for its great success. I therefore recommend it highly.

A. Jesus' Method of Choice

Jesus is the original founder of personal evangelism as it is recorded in the New Testament. After recruiting His twelve disciples, He appointed seventy-two others (in addition to the twelve) and sent them in pairs ahead of Him to every town and village where He was about to go. He told them "the harvest is plentiful, but the workers are few" (Luke 10:1-2). The Lord knew the best method to invite individuals to the ministry was by personal evangelism method. No wonder He approached seven out of the twelve of His disciples individually. He further personally led the Samaritan woman to salvation (John 4:25-29), after which she was so joyful that she enthusiastically invited her whole village to meet Christ. In addition to the Samaritan woman, Jesus also evangelised the Rabbi Nicodemus who was converted by night when he understood the need to be born again -- born of the spirit (John 3:3). "Zacchaeus, come down immediately, I must stay at your house today" (Luke 19:5) are Jesus' invitation words to a sinner who was seeking a new life. Examples could be multiplied. The point we are making is that for best results, nothing can replace personal evangelism, a method used to invite so many to Christ in the first century, and I believe it is still effective in the twenty-first century, and will always be.

In addition to the fact that it is a proven, effective method of winning persons to Christ and His Church, there is one other very special quality about personal evangelism; that is anyone, who is willing to apply it, can do so. It is user friendly because actually it is God working through any willing "disciple". Yes, the only criterion is *"willingness to go and teach or testify"* that Jesus Christ is Lord.

In spite of this, there are still Christians who give such excuses as, "It is the preacher's business to witness. He/she is the one who is paid to do that." That is nothing but a lame and naked excuse. This is wrong. In fact such an attitude is not consistent with the Christian spirit. This attitude is found among Christians who assign visiting the sick to the doctors and nurses, feeding the hungry to the State welfare programs, visiting the prisoners to the Warden, etc. When the Son of man comes, as recorded in the gospels, such people may be shocked (Matt. 25:31-46). In his book *Revolution in Evangelism*, W. Dayton Roberts said, "a church which bottlenecks its outreach by depending on its specialities, its pastor or evangelist to do its witnessing is living in violation of both the intention of its head (Christ) and the consistent pattern of the early Christians" (Roberts, 1980, 97). So clearly, everyone must witness, testify, evangelise.

B. The Early Church's Victorious Style

Christian witnesses who turned the Roman Empire right side up were not ordained men and women, but simple, some uneducated, Christian men and women who were obedient and spirit-filled. They were moved by their passion for the gospel. In *Taking Men Alive*, Charles G. Trumbell says, "the work of individual soul winning is the greatest work that God permits men (to want) to do. It was Christ's own preferred method of work, it is His preferred method for us today, for it is always the most effective way of working" (Trumbell, 1980,7).

Admittedly the business of winning souls to Christ is not an easy one. The challenge is upon those who confess Jesus Christ as Lord. Trumbell continues, "individual soul winning is not easy, it is hard. It is the hardest work that God asks us to do for Him" (Ibid). What else is important and golden in this world, that is easy to get? Cheap things, yes. But God's work of winning souls is not cheap. Each and every soul is precious and must be fought for. That is why Jesus prayed: "My Father if possible, may this cup be taken from me. Yet not as I will but as you will" (Matt. 26:39). Most of the disciples died or were killed for preaching the gospel. Numerous martyrs are counted today. But that is how the gospel reached us in Africa today. It took some courageous laity and clergy to spread the gospel. I repeat: some may say it is hard but those who are committed to Christ can do it.

C. My Personal Experience as Pastor and Evangelist

One of the wonderful things about witnessing is that the more one witnesses, the more one becomes spiritually enriched. Therefore those who do not witness may actually be starving their souls spiritually. Whereas, in the world of materialism, if we have three loaves of bread and we give away two, we remain with only one, in the spiritual realm, (that is witnessing),the more you share your love, your grace and testimony, the more you are not only spiritually enriched but also blessed with Christian joy. By the way, this is why after preaching we always leave the pulpit full of joy! That is the proven result of sharing the love of Christ.

When I was the Conference Assistant Director of Evangelism -- during the Rhodesia days, I assisted a missionary from Oneanta, Alabama, the Rev. Dr. M.J. Murphree who was a down to earth evangelist. The personal evangelism method worked amazingly well for us then as it did during Jesus' time, St. Paul's era, and it is still the most effective, I believe. One of the reasons I like it is because it is suitable for use on anybody. I have found that simple people, sophisticated people, the rich or the poor, black or white, all respond well to this method. It is convert friendly. Jesus loves them all and He wants them into the fold by all means. In each case, the statement: "Jesus loves you" always seems to trigger a peculiar sense of dependence and worth in the sight of God. The statement speaks almost to every heart.

Allow me to share with you what I actually heard, saw, said and did as an evangelist in Zimbabwe: what worked for me. Of course, I often teamed up with the lay leader or some church member. In an evangelistic campaign, one day after we had followed all the procedures to prepare the volunteer trainees to evangelise, (which I will discuss later), the time had come to go out to meet the unchurched. It was time for people to voluntarily choose whom they felt comfortable visiting in the region. After completing a survey of the targeted region, we followed Jesus' method of sending them in two's for maximum effect. Generally we preferred that men visited male prospects, while women visited females, youths to youths. Everything went well as planned and hoped, until a problem suddenly arose. Our list had the name of a man nobody had the courage to visit. It took us time and a little bit of struggle to try and persuade a pair of men to go visit this particular individual. Then a strange thing happened: two women decided to volunteer to visit the man! When that happened, I immediately knew that something big -- something unusual and divine-driven was about to happen.

Now this individual was huge of stature; also he was one of the wealthiest and highly educated people in the community. Being a "backslider" with some issues, he was bitter towards the church. Everybody was afraid of him, so when these two women volunteered to visit him, it had to be an act of faith -- the work of the Holy Spirit. Having made an exception to the rule of gender matching, we sent off these two brave women to visit this potential troublemaker. In a culture that is male-dominated, for these women to volunteer to approach this man was simply daring. We had to trust that the hand of the Holy Spirit would be at work.

After a lot of praying in the bush on their way, they would have been disappointed if they did not find him home. Fortunately they found the man at home. According to our visitation practice, they asked to speak to him separately from his family. After introducing themselves, they shared their testimonies of what the Lord had done for them. They told him "Jesus loves you." Then they invited him to join them in prayer. First they prayed for him, then asked him to pray, too. To summarize his prayer, the man groaned, tears on his cheeks: "Lord Jesus thank you for sending 'Mary and Martha' to raise me, a 'Lazarus,' dead in sin and sinking in the grave." He also confessed many things he felt were not right before God. Penitent and broken-hearted, following his own prayer, the man gave his testimony; that was indeed the miracle.

That very evening, he came to church and did what few people do these days, especially in the West. He sat in the front pew and had a chance to give his testimony, in front of the entire congregation. He said he had been lost and that Jesus had reclaimed him through the witness of the two women whom he figuratively named "Martha and Mary", Lazarus' sisters. He himself was the Lazarus whom Jesus brought back to life (John 11:43-44). The two women felt very humbled by how God had used them to save a perishing soul. They were in the highest of spirits, full of joy from being pleasantly surprised. They were convinced that it was not by their own wisdom, ability, might or power, but through the Holy Spirit that they were triumphant.

In evaluating this glorious example of a successful mission, it is important to appreciate that the two women had very little training and zero experience. Their only real preparation was the prayers offered prior to arrival. As we pointed out earlier on, the Holy Spirit does all the hard work in this method. Such is the *divine driven power of personal evangelism.*

D. Polity versus the Holy Spirit

Another incident I can remember happened back in 1956, in what they now call Makoni Central (then Chiduku North Circuit) of Zimbabwe. I was the pastor serving a 16-point charge covering an area about 30 square-miles (77 square-kilometres). I travelled from point to point by bicycle, for public transport was very scarce and unreliable. The nearest church was three miles (5 kilometres) from the parsonage at Muziti, and the farthest was over 20 miles (32 kilometres) away at Chizawana. People often ask me how did I do it?[13] Now this is what happened on one occasion in my circuit. I asked the late Mr. Matthew Chabarwa Mataranyika, a very dedicated Christian and headmaster of the school where I lived, to team up with me. Together we would visit the famous Mr. Toto, who in addition to being the village head, was a renowned herbalist (traditional healer) as well as a revered polygamist. Our mission was to tell him about Jesus Christ. Fortunately he only lived six miles (nine and half kilometres)

---

[13] How did God's work get done? There were 45 laymen and women who did the work of witnessing as I itinerated among the 16 churches plus some preaching points. I aimed to visit each one regularly and after three months the cycle would start again. Today, the same geographic area has been divided into seven circuits. Still the pastor depends on the service of the dedicated Christian lay people. Many people who ask about the secret of the fastest growing church in Africa may want to know that among other things, we can identify lay people who have accepted Jesus Christ as their saviour, who are more than happy to share their faith with others.

away from the parsonage. So we cycled there.

We humbly asked to see him alone. After giving our testimonies and telling him that God loved him and that our mission was precisely to share the good news with him, we took turns to pray, and then asked him to say something to God who was present with us and was listening to our conversation. With appropriate words, he accepted Jesus Christ that very hour.

The following day at about 5 a.m., someone was knocking on my door. When I opened the door, my first reaction was that there must be a disaster because generally speaking herbalists do not venture far from home unless they are in search of rare herbs, or if they are asked to treat a bed-ridden patient. Though over 80 years old, Mr. Toto, the village icon, had walked the six miles to the parsonage because, according to him, he had had a "sleepless night." After exchanging customary greetings in Shona *"Warara here?"* (Did you sleep well?) *"Ndarara, kuti wararawo"* (I slept well, if you slept well.) He sighed heavily, then said: "I have come to be baptized. I accepted Jesus whom you told me about yesterday when you came to my home." Wow!

Needless to say, I was pleased, excited, surprised and thanked God, and yet I am sorry to say, I was also caught between the bureaucracy [polity] of the Methodist Church and acceding to the request. The bureaucracy won. I explained to him that I had to enrol him in the Beginners' class and baptize him months later.

Disappointed, he left the parsonage and went right to the nearest Roman Catholic priest who baptized him promptly because he had made up his mind to be a Christian, and was convinced that he should be baptized. The following year, Mr. Toto fell sick and died! At least I was consoled to know that he had accepted Jesus Christ. Needless to say, if I knew then what I know now, I should have baptized him there and then though the church hierarchy would most likely penalize me for it.

E. Evangelising -- Step by Step [How do *you* do it?]

Personal evangelism is not haphazard. There are certain guiding principles or procedures in preparing for the amazing harvest of souls. What I share here are just some of what has worked for others and me. This is not written in stone.

1st Step. Spiritual Preparation:

Both the preacher/evangelist and the pastor/leader prepare themselves to do the work of evangelism. The pastor preaches a series of evangelistic messages inviting Christians to the task of loving other people as God "has loved us" and bringing them to Christ. I believe that bringing people to Christ is not the same as bringing them to church. The emphasis must be 'Christ', not 'church'. When they accept Jesus they will come to church naturally. Some of the more obvious Scripture passages to preach from are" Gen. 3:9; Is. 6:8; Matt. 5:13-14; Matt. 28:19-20; Luke 9:1-6; 10:1-20; 15:1-31; 19:10; John 20:21; John 3:16-18, etc. Of course the whole Bible is full of messages relating to God's invitation to humanity that has gone astray.

Just be cognisant of the socio-political context.

2nd Step. Survey:

Conduct a regional survey of the community to determine how many people in that constituency are within your reach, should they decide to come to church. Of course people who do not belong to any church are most ideal candidates for evangelism. Also there may be some who used to come to church but, for whatever reason, have since stopped coming. Try to identify their status, condition and anticipate their needs. Think through their situation until you understand their life experience that led them to where they are today. This "homework" helps you in many ways including your recruiting strategies. Prayerfully, make *a list* of the names of those whom you will approach. One should always be subject to the guidance of the Holy Spirit.

3rd Step. Prayer:

Now is time for the congregation to pray for the prospects. Pray for sometime -- say four weeks. You can take your time. The Lord takes His time to answer prayer, but I believe that He answers every single prayer. Pray as individuals, in teams and as the whole congregation being of one accord with the mind of Christ. Pray that the Lord will open the minds of all those you have targeted to visit so they welcome your approach, hear your message and have the rare opportunity to receive God's love [conversion]! Pray for your list. Pray that God's will be done -- to save the lost -- which is what Jesus came on earth to do. "For the Son of man came to seek and to save what was lost" (Luke 19:10). Furthermore, He promised that if we pray according to His will, He would answer such prayers.

4th Step. Train the evangelism team:

Ask your church-members to volunteer to be trained how to witness and invite people to Christ. Train them to witness effectively and approach the unchurched with respect. They have the love, spirit and the willingness to share. All they need is some clues and pointers of how to witness effectively. As I have shared earlier Jesus is ahead of His people who desire to seek the lost. During the training sessions, you may need to have some role play (especially for new volunteers) to dramatize what could happen during an actual visit, being sure to cover these approach scenarios:

1. ...to *a non-believer (atheist)* -- "The fool says in his heart 'there is no God'" (Ps. 14:1). But this is probably not the Scripture one would use.
2. ...to *a backslider*. Think about the arguments they usually put up and set up. For example someone may have disappointed them at church (perhaps the pastor), perhaps they were hurt or simply fell back, craving attention, lay-leadership discontent.
3. ...to *old people and their special circumstances*, e.g. in Africa where they know there is a God, but do not know about Jesus. Think about

their respective needs and situation.
4. ...to *doubters (sceptics)*
5. ...to *agnostics* who say they don't know if it is possible to know anything for certain about God
6. ...to the *lost "liberals,"* who are proud and think they are too sophisticated to believe in the Jesus experience instead of science or other science-oriented knowledge.

With special reference to Zimbabwe, one would also add the following also:

7. We emphasized that the whole exercise must not take more than 20 minutes.
8. We emphasized that never, ever argue, raise your voice, be annoyed, agitated or stay if you feel threatened. If the testifying leads to arguments, quickly close and try to come back another time.
9. Never make judgemental comments. Although sometimes one may actually tell you that he or she is a sinner with bad habits, it is best not to pursue that topic. Emphasize that Jesus loves them and urge them, to give themselves to him. Don't go on to tell them to stop swearing, drinking, adultery, etc. I know some churches that preach the "don'ts." I say, do not focus on the negative.
10. If and when they have accepted Jesus, pray for them and invite him or her to say something to Jesus in a meaningful prayer. If they say they don't know what to say, then it is your golden opportunity to lead with a short poignant prayer.

Finally, the training must be concluded with words of assurance that the Holy Spirit has 'already gone ahead of us." Jesus says, " Lo, I am with you always" (Matt. 28:20). Tell the trainees that the main point is sharing what God is doing among us -- real life experience issues. In addition, in the long term, it is advisable that trainees attend Bible study regularly.

5th Step. Spiritual Guidance:

Before leaving, pray once more. Ask the Holy Spirit to go ahead of you and talk to Mr. Gashirai or Mrs. Gashirai -- by name. Don't forget your Bible. You may never get to use it, but it will come in handy when situations necessitate reading the written word. Remember how Jesus used Scripture in His ministry, against Satan for example (Matt. 4:4-10). It is recommended that one knows *by heart* the Bible verses one intends to use.

6th Step. Face to Face:

Now you are face to face with Mr. Gashirai or Mrs. Gashirai; in a friendly manner, introduce yourselves by name/s, where you are from[14] --

---

[14] I do not recommend that you introduce yourself as coming from any particular part of the country or region. Whereas this should make no difference, it may shift the focus of your primary mission in the mind of the prospect. It should be adequate to simply state which church you are from.

your church/denomination. In a very polite fashion, ask if you can have a word with him/her very briefly. You may identify where you worship. But whether or not you do, be sure to emphasize that Jesus Christ has sent you to visit him or her. I know many people find it easier to say their church has sent them, but in my view, that weakens your case. Placing emphasis on having been sent by Jesus will make your introduction more attractive, authoritative, affirmative and irrefutable when you say "Jesus sent us to tell you Mr Gashirai that He loves you". Then you have opened his/her heart to love of Jesus in His praise. (N.B.: Backsliders especially have a problem with the church but very few people have problem with Jesus. Make them understand from the outset that He who sent you is greater than the church, the pastor, the Bishop).

7th Step. Own Testimony:

At this point you may share your testimonies. For example, who Jesus is, who God is and what He means to you. What He has done for you most recently: not from 15 or 25 years ago, but recently. It is generally not very effective to talk about what happened to you many years ago, but of course *it is your personal conversation:* the testimony may actually be very persuasive.

It is important to realise the importance of this testimony you are giving. For a long time to come, what you share will be the reference point for this convert. The words will resonate in his head as he plays back over and over again -- the moment the Holy Spirit convicted him and he was converted. Hence it is very important to plan carefully what to share and how to share it. A lot rides on your own testimony. Plan it. Rehearse it. Revisit it. Perfect it. Deliver it -- with good effect -- confidently. This is not the moment to search for the right word to use or stutter. However remember, if this should happen, the Holy Spirit is backing you.

8th Step. The Invitation:

In the story of a young man I met in a railway waiting room at Bromley, near Harare, Zimbabwe, which we discussed in chapter three, I used another formula, but I still concluded by appealing to the man to accept Christ

Armstrong suggests: "... speak from the heart, not from the head. Feel sincerity in what you say, or (else) don't say it. Let the person know how you feel, not what you think...identify with the other person in his or her struggle, pain, doubt" (Armstrong, 1979, 95). If you are asked a question you can't answer, be honest to say, "I don't know. I shall ask my pastor".

In our Zimbabwe experience we found that each team found their own words. If you answer some questions by Scripture it is more effective and convincing.

It is vitally important that you end your testimony by inviting them to accept Jesus. A most moving testimony can flop if you do not utter words to invite Mr or Mrs Gashirai to *accept Jesus*. Indeed, the Holy Spirit is with you but *you*, the evangelist, must utter those words. Failure to do so, at that crucial moment, may make the difference between someone being saved and condemning them to continued life in the wilderness. Say it.

9th Step. Prayer:

The Holy Spirit will step in to convict and a convert is made in God's good time. (One of the mistakes some people make is to be over eager to see the effects of this statement. They will repeat it over and over hoping to see a sudden change. I want to remind you that God's timetable of events is too complex for our human schema. Remember, evangelism that decolonizes the soul is a partnership with Christ. The evangelist does their part, trust the Holy Spirit will do His.)

If they accept Jesus on the spot, then *pray* together -- invite them to 'say' something to God in Jesus' name. If not, move on. The Holy Spirit will continue evangelising them long afterwards.

10th Step. Invitation to Attend Church:

You invited them to accept Jesus; you invited them to say something to Jesus; now invite them to come to your church service and take down their name, address and phone number. Assure them that you will be looking for them at church on Sunday. They can count on you being there.

11th Step. Personal Testimony:

When they come to church, ask if they want to say a word of testimony in public. This is a very important way of anchoring, and strengthening one's faith. It is also an encouragement for the disciples who have been praying that God may be bringing new converts. In countries and cultures that emphasize "time" and "privacy" more than Jesus, they may not want to share personal testimonies. That is quite all right too, but you must at least give them this crucial first opportunity to anchor their faith. This strengthens their resolve and commitment to the decision they have just reached and makes immediate backtracking harder for them. Don't lose this chance. Don't deny them this chance. It could make all the difference between a short-lived resolution and a long-term commitment. Indeed, this is the jurisdiction of the pastor. However the evangelist team that visited Mr. and Mrs. Gashirai will need to bring the convert to the attention of the pastor who will find time for the personal testimony in that day's service.

12th Step. Reporting:

The members who went out to witness will give a report of how their mission was. If there were some negative and discouraging reports, they are reserved for pastor's ears only. But generally, a majority of the reports are encouraging. Remember when the 72 whom Jesus sent in two's came back to report to Jesus; it is said "the seventy returned with joy and said "Lord, even the demons submitted to us in your name" (Luke 10:17).

Dr. Alan Walker, Australian born world evangelist says, "There is no satisfaction on earth to equal the sheer gladness of a heart that comes with sharing in the bringing of another person into the kingdom of heaven" (Walker, 1980, 92). In Bolivia, Latin America, in a national program called "Evangelism in Depth," among those who went out, a woman reported back, "We went out to visit. I went with fear. I did not know what they would say. Tears ran down my face that day because eight persons, of those that I visited, gave their hearts to the Lord. Now we have new courage" (Roberts, 1980, 118). By the way, some evangelists prefer to see prospects as families in their home. I prefer that you focus on each family member individually. There is a positive effect in knowing that you are the person to whom Jesus is talking -- personally and directly.

13th Step. Organized evangelism celebration:

Organize, if you can afford it, a celebrative preaching and fellowship service with new members in attendance to anchor and strengthen them in the faith. It is also spiritual nourishment for those who did the visitations. Truly, there is joy in heaven over one sinner who repents! Similarly, there is celebration in the church by those who visited, and their hearts are filled with joy, delight and blessings. Celebrate! Rejoice! Exult!

Finally, let me say in Africa, pastors should plan to visit in the homes of their new converts, even prospects. It is great! Outside Africa, especially in the West, one needs to know who appreciates visitation in their homes, and who does not because some just do not appreciate home visits. If you really desire and wish, you could have new members. What are you waiting for? Personal evangelism method is your ticket! Start using it immediately! May the grace of the Lord Jesus Christ, the love of God, and the fellowship of the Holy Spirit be with you."

II. SITUATIONAL EVANGELISM

Situational evangelism appears to be very casual, yet if the message is "evangelistic" it could touch individual souls in a special manner. How can you learn to recognize an opportunity for evangelism?

The story is told of three men walking by a stadium that was packed to capacity with spectators. The first man walked by and thought, if only I could get all these people to vote for me in the next election. The second one walked by and thought, if I just had about twenty minutes to preach the gospel concluding with an altar call, I am sure someone would accept Christ -- someone would be saved today. The third one walked by and thought, "all those wallets and purses just waiting to be snatched."

We can tell what each one did for a living from what the crowd caused them to imagine. What would have been your first thought at the sight of such a multitude? In Africa in general, Zimbabwe in particular, opportunities for evangelism present themselves every day, everywhere. Be constantly on the look out for a captive audience, even if the audience is as small as two or three people because Jesus Christ said where two or three are gathered "in my name, I am in their midst" (Matt. 18:20). Let us now examine various occasions where evangelism can happen.

A. At Funerals

When Maggie and I lost our second born son, Philemon in 1998, literally thousands of mourners came to console us. This immediately presented us with an opportunity to evangelise both the unchurched and backsliders. So, worship services were scheduled at regular intervals because we wanted to be sure that the gospel was preached...that we offered life in Jesus Christ in the very presence of death. Over the three-day mourning period, several people were blessed and spiritually rejuvenated in the several worship services that were held.

In 2003, Mrs. Martha Mudzengere, the widow of one of our dear prominent preachers, lost her daughter and a son within 48 hours of each other. I was asked to preach at one of the funerals. After delivering the sermon, I invited people to Christ. Three women came forward and one of them said: "From today I want to join the United Methodist Church. I was Roman Catholic". The other two converts simply accepted Christ for the first time. Yes, mourners need to hear the word of God who comforts the bereaved, heals the sick and simply ministers and restores souls. To be honest, I don't regard changing from one denomination to another as conversion. All the same, our point here is that some people make major religious decisions at funerals.

At yet another occasion in Makoni district, at the funeral of one of my nieces -- Nurse Magosha -- we witnessed the conversion of six women who accepted Christ in response to a moving, powerful message. We could go on and on listing incidents of mourners getting converted at funerals because the speakers at these occasions now know that there is no better moment to preach God's gift of eternal life at funerals, when one's mortality and clinging onto life is on everyone's mind.

Our culture has a way of bringing together all sorts of people: church people of different denominations, non-believers, men, women, and youth, the educated and the uneducated, the poor and the rich. Also this is where the backsliders from different denominations present themselves readily. Gathered to mourn, and puzzled by the mystery of death, people become vulnerable as they realise how easily and quickly life can end. This is the time to preach evangelistic messages. There is no more suitable time to offer Jesus, who is the way, the truth and *the life*. No wonder in *Death and the Life After,* Dr. Billy Graham says, "A funeral sermon is not for the dead, but those who are still in the physical world" (Graham, 1988). Because in our culture people are expected to gather for some days at the home of the bereaved in order to comfort them, attendance at the worship services is always guaranteed. However, since some people must go back to work during the day, evenings are most ideal for holding organized worship services. As I look into the future, I see a need to structure these services to the Lord's better advantage. By this I mean, lots of people will plan to go and offer their condolences at a time that will coincide with a worship service. Perhaps we should study how we can make these services more responsive to these people. The fact that they come just in time for the service and are gone immediately afterwards suggest that there may be a special common thread or need that can be ministered to.

Friends and nuclear relatives (especially daughters-in-law and sons-in-law) are required to stay throughout; they do all the catering, assisted by extended family. Yes. The bereaved do the catering. But since the church is our family, it is not unusual to find church groups catering to the hundreds or thousands of mourners, especially if the deceased belonged to a Section.

In a sense, funerals are also a "social event" insofar as family will get together in its extended version, not just the nuclear family. There is a degree of socializing mixed with deep sense of loss. Paying ones last respects entails intermittent mourning. Indeed the situation renders itself a revival, especially when the Holy Spirit is allowed to manifest Himself through singing, dancing, praying and even fellowshipping. Generally speaking, whenever and wherever there are gatherings like this, disciples should be alert for opportunities to present evangelism that decolonizes the sin-sick souls in society.

B. At Weddings

Let us take advantage of the merriment for evangelising. After the bride and groom have exchange vows, there is always a time for congratulatory speeches, wrongly called *umbowo, (Testimonies)*. These are not all testimonies because, by definition, a "testimony" is when one shares what one heard, saw or did in the context of the Holy Spirit. At any rate, in the world which is sick and stinking of failed relationships between husbands and wives, brothers and their sisters, cousins and neighbours, sermons based on Christian relationship may lead to salvation for some. Scriptures like Romans 12:9-21; 1 Corinthians 13:1-13; 1 John 4:7-12; may be suitable choices to guide the thinking of the crowd. Also there is ample opportunity to preach about forgiveness and reconciliation in this setting. The occasion begs for such messages .The world would be different if husbands and wives and cousins just tried to forgive as Christ taught and actually did. Living by the golden rule (Matt. 7:12) would draw many to Christ because often times love is contagious. Exploit the situation as Jesus did when He "saw the multitude...sat down to teach them."

C. In Crisis

In general, people suffer in different ways. Diseases, unemployment, psychological abuse or outright violence and other hostile circumstances cause many to suffer, often times needlessly. When Christians offer, in Jesus' name, to visit such individuals, just the visit alone could decolonize a soul that has been captive for years. Jesus simply summed up His mission when He said: "I have come so they may have life and have it abundantly." Most will agree that people who are suffering tend to be very vulnerable. On the one hand history has examples of those who got converted in times of suffering, but on the other hand, some have actually left the fold on account of what they perceived as meaningless suffering. John Newton is a good example of one who experienced a dramatic turn around because he got converted on a stormy night that threatened lives of all the people who were on the boat with him. Frightened by this storm at sea, he promised God that if he survived the storm, he would accept and follow Christ. He was spared and all at once SAVED. Consistent with his promise, Newton later became a minister of religion with the influence and with the help of John Wesley and George Whitefield. Subsequently, he composed three hundred hymns. Today most of us enjoy the hymns he wrote including the all time favourite which is now sung all over the world: "Amazing Grace...How sweet the sound... That saved a wretch like me." *(Tsitsi Dzinondishamisa, Hymn 178, Ngoma dzeUMC yeZimbabwe)* -- the testimony of his salvation. The words spell his celebration of God's grace that plucked him from the error of his former ways. In a way, it is everyone's testimony too. The only problem here is that a lot of us just enjoy singing this hymn and other hymns like it, but we have never experienced what it means to be saved by *God's grace alone.*

There is a different type of crisis in beer halls. I wish God would raise more committed laypersons, pastors, and evangelists who can confidently dare risk their reputation by visiting places like the beer halls where many souls are experiencing spiritual and sometimes moral decay because their souls are captured by the evil one. The sheer number of people who are trying to drink their problems away is amazing. A sizeable number just need someone to show them some acceptance and tolerances -- simply by telling them, "Jesus loves you." Yes, 'daring' is the word because there are social stigmas that go with "a minister of religion in the beer hall ". What business does he or she have socializing with *chidhakwa* (drunk or an alcoholic -- singular)? The same sort of accusation was levelled at Jesus when He mingled with "tax collectors, prostitutes and sinners". But we can more easily win their friendship if we accept *zvidhakwa* (plural) as persons like us with the exception that we do not have to drink liquor to the point of being enslaved by the habit.

Some clergy have a hard time deciding what funeral rituals to use when they bury chidhakwa, but do not experience the same when they bury a "church member" even if he or she broke all the ten commandments during one's life on earth. They figure, as long as the individual wore the church uniform, worshipped with us, then never mind that the person was alleged to be a witch or other sin. Such clergy get preoccupied whether or not to pronounce the words: *"Ivhu kuivhu, dota kudota, mweya unodzokera kuna Mwari uyo akaupa* "(Dust to dust, ashes to ashes, and the spirit returns to God who gave it,) when burying the *chidhakwa.* There is serious confused theological thinking here. When are we going to learn that a person is not a Christian just because he or she does not drink liquor and or smoke tobacco. Adolf Hitler did not drink or smoke even though he did cause the murder of six million Jews. Would we regard him as a saint just because he was not a *chidhakwa*?

My belief is that we should let *zvidhakwa* come to church as they are and join the saved sinners who have uniforms and sashes in the church. God can meet them there with His grace, along with the rest. After all, there are clergy, laymen and laywomen, suited up to the hilt, who have been in the church for a long time, are good at giving their tithes, do not miss going to church on Sundays [or on Saturday for their Sabbath Observance], but don't practice the real, true Christian spirit of love, forgiveness and making peace and offering sacrificial services which are the mark of a true Christian. True Christians are marked by "fruits and spirit of love, joy, peace, patience, kindness, goodness, faithfulness, gentleness and self control," [Galatians 5:22] not by not drinking or smoking. In case some one may misunderstand me, I want to be clear, I hate drinking and smoking tobacco because they are destructive habits. I detest the habit, but I do not hate the people who do it. Equally I hate the misguided idea that the only mark of a Christian is not drinking liquor, smoking tobacco and other substance abuse.

Another captive audiences are the people who come to the hospital to care for their hospitalised relatives. They are sad, afraid and anxious about what will happen to their dear ones. Frankly, they are worried. Furthermore it is hard to visit the sick in many hospitals in Africa where so many have marginal care and facilities that are not up to par. In addition, when one visits the hospital, inevitably one comes out both worried and thankful that "but for the grace of God, I could be the one in the hospital bed." I am sure that hospital visitors have had that sense and feeling at one time or another, wherever in the world you may be. But in order to fully understand why the visitor needs our attention as much as the patient in the hospital bed, let us examine what other factors come to bear on the hospital visitor.

Often visitors leave home before sunrise in order to arrive at the hospital on time for the early morning visiting time. They help feed and bathe the patient. At the end of the period, they leave the wards and the hospital building but they do not go home, for a variety of reasons e.g. because they have come too far and it will take too long or cost too much to get back home and return for another visit that day or the next day. Perhaps they stay because they have been saving for weeks or months just to visit this once. So, for whatever reasons, they find a shady spot and wait for the next visiting time, four or five hours later, after which, indeed they return to the shade until the evening visiting time. They may eventually get home late at night or they may just campout all night near the hospital -- tomorrow is yet another day.

Each time they are in the presence of the patient, the visitor cannot let their concern show especially when the prognosis of their loved one is bleak. Some visitors are breadwinners who cannot afford the recommended treatment. Doctors have prescribed medicines that the Pharmacists do not stock. Dispensary shelves are bare. The drugs may be too expensive or may only be available abroad -- beyond reach. The point is they have physical demands -- fatigue, as well as the mental demands -- concern, weighing them down. So they need support themselves.

How can we serve the visitors? Find a way, with consultations with hospital authorities, to bring the good news to them together with their patients. Let St. James give them this counsel in these words.

> "Is any one of you in trouble? He should pray. Is any one happy? Let him sing songs of praise. Is any one of you sick? He should call an elder of the church to pray over him, anoint him with oil in the name of the Lord and the prayer offered in faith will make the sick person well. The Lord will raise him up. If he has sinned, he will be forgiven. Therefore confess your sins to each other and pray for each other so that you may be healed" [James 5:13-16].

Let me conclude by saying one needs special skills to deal with terminally ill patients and their visitors. There is indeed such a thing as a denial ministry that offers wrongful hope, (not to be confused with false hope). Minister appropriately.

D. Professionals

George Hunter III would call this the "stability" category in society. They feel they need nothing because they are comfortable materially. They are what we would call the "defiance of God " category. Interestingly, among the professionals there are some who occupy the highest offices in society. In Africa, unfortunately some pastors get cold feet in approaching them with the gospel. Some high-ranking officials have never been to church, not even at Christmas or Easter. It has been too long ago when they got baptized in church, and they will be dead when their body is taken to church for their funeral. The only time they want priests [ministers of religion], is when they want pulpit time because they need a large audience during the election year and when they need a man or woman of God to pronounce *"ivhu kuivhu "* [dust to dust] when their bodies are lowered in the grave.

Priests and other religious leaders must visit them while they are still living. Ask them to commit themselves to Jesus Christ. Why not? Most people want to go to heaven, so let us offer them Christ, the Saviour. They should know and acknowledge " *Baba/Mai, we zveMweya* " [father/mother of spiritual affairs]. If you follow all the steps and procedures we have suggested in this book, you can't fail. The Holy Spirit will help you bring some one to Christ in spite of yourself. Do not feel inferior to talk or witness to politicians, rich government officials about Christ and the church. You are an important messenger of God. You are superior in Jesus' name. One of the methods to evangelise the "stability " is to give them some responsibility in church.

E. Companions of Opportunity

We have already related the story of how I met a man at Bromley while we were both waiting for a train. We were thrown together unexpectedly and by this chance meeting, salvation came his way. Many such chance encounters can occur daily if we are tuned-in spiritually to the people around us as they go about their business and we go about ours.

We spend a good part of each day waiting for one thing or another in some public place. We wait in banks, doctors' reception areas, at sporting events, for public transport or a fuel queue and airport departure lounges. Unwittingly we become companions with those waiting with us, even though they are total strangers. These are daily opportunities to evangelise. Here is a good illustration.

Retired United Methodist clergyman, Reverend Fanuel Kadenge is my best friend. He shares a moving incident which showcases opportune situational evangelism. I believe that Fanuel is deeply saturated with the Holy Spirit because he will do whatever he feels moved to do by the Holy Spirit.

One day while on the bus, he was sitting behind this total stranger when "Suddenly I felt a real strong urge to pray for him so that the Lord would save him," he says. Who was this person? Just a stranger who was sitting in the seat in front of him on a bus. Understandably, Fanuel hesitated as most of us often do when we feel nudged by the Holy Spirit. But due to the pressure or urging he felt to pray for this person, Fanuel decided to pray quietly within himself. Without a single word being uttered, suddenly the man spun around and looked at Fanuel, who was in clergy outfit. It was as though someone had tapped him on the shoulder from behind. By the way, Fanuel never closes his eyes when he prays, so their eyes met immediately. Had the spirit of peace not already united the two men, i.e. the Holy Spirit, who knows what discussion might have ensued.

"I felt you touch me, " the stranger said.

Fanuel asked: " Do you know Jesus ?"

The two gazed at each other for a moment before the agitated stranger replied: "No". Fanuel gave his testimony to this stranger, relating who Jesus is and asked God to save this man. He told the man that he was praying for him and that the touch he felt must be God reaching out to embrace him in His love. According to Fanuel, *the man was converted right there on the commuter bus.* This story reminds most evangelists of Phillip and the Ethiopian eunuch [Acts 8:29-39]. Although Fanuel did not baptize this man on the bus, I am sure the man received spiritual baptism in his heart.

F. Taking Jesus to the Bank

During my years in resident episcopal administration, the United Methodist Church had the tradition of celebrating what they called the "Social Hour" on the final Saturday afternoon of the weekend of the Annual Conference. This time was set aside for entertainment and relaxation.[15] Of the twenty-four years I was in office, I will never forget the year we had invited two highly placed clergy persons from the Anglican Church and the Church of Christ to represent their denominations. Since my chair was next to theirs, I could not help but overhear their conversation.

---

[15] Actually, originally this tradition started as "The Bishop's Reception".

"Yes, she is the one. Yes, that tall one. She is the one." They were pointing at a tall, lean, young woman who was performing on the stage. I became curious about this woman and since I asked the two men, they excitedly drew me in their conversation:

"Bishop, do you see that tall and lean woman?"

"Yes." I replied.

"That lady takes Jesus to the Standard Chartered Bank."

"Exactly what do you mean ?" I inquired.

"She works at the Standard Chartered Bank 'X' Branch and she treats people, talks, serves and relates to people with a Christian attitude and spirit. She takes her Jesus with her to the bank." One of them explained.

Here is a living example of a person who lives her faith. "A great effective one!" we all agreed. The bank's clients who come in contact with her at work must not only feel but also think about the meaning of "Christian" without her mentioning the words "Jesus" or "church ". True, bankers are trained to be friendly to their customers but this woman does more than the usual: she practises "Christian customer service ".

There are subliminal situations all around us -- at home, at work, yes even at church or any gatherings where, through our true Christian lives, other people can be blessed and can be touched and influenced. Living a genuine Christian life that is contagious is a very powerful and effective method of evangelising.

G. With Jesus in the Devil's Den

Some years ago I read about some very disturbing behaviour of a professional individual. This man, in my opinion, did not belong in the academia. He was a university lecturer in West Africa. He had this habit of asking his female students to cook for him. They were put on a roster so they would go on duty at certain days of school hours. After she had prepared his meal, the lecturer demanded sex. This went on for some time until one day he ran into a Holy calamity in the person of Tote who would not succumb to that immorality.

After she finished her work and she said 'Good night,' the man expected his routine crime. When the rapist told her she could not go before she had sex with him, then Tote told him off. When he advanced towards her she said: "If you move one more step towards me, I will scream for help". The lecturer said: "All other girls do it with me. " She retorted, "If they do it, go to them then, not me! I do not do that kind of stuff." She slammed the door in his face and dashed off to her home.

The following day the lecturer had the nerve to call Tote again and told her: "All the girls who come to cook for me will have sex with me before they leave; why did you act silly yesterday?" To this, the girl replied boldly, "I am a Christian, and the only man who shall have sex with me is one who shall have stood side by side with me in front of a minister of religion at the altar." Tote made her Christian values clear regarding sex before marriage. The lecturer was challenged by the answer " ... because I am a Christian". Being a pagan, the lecturer was almost shocked, then he said to Tote: "If being a Christian makes even a little girl as courageous as this, I also want to be a Christian". For the purpose of this book, it suffices to say this is another classic example of evangelism that decolonizes persons, by example.

III. THE FISHING GOES ON [Matt. 4:19]

Chapter Six describes the gospel network. The fishing metaphor we use in this chapter goes back to Jesus' own words to the disciples: "I will make you fishers of men (sic) people." So we have chosen to discuss evangelism using "netting" as the central motif.

When I go fishing, (usually on Monday), I feel it is more prudent to cast two or three lines at once because one never knows which will have a bite first. Often I will put different bait on each line to assess the situation. In witnessing to catch people for Christ we have a variety of ways to win converts. Therefore, we do well to try several ways and contexts within which to evangelise. The most usual ways are: the family, schools/institutions, secular meetings, crusades, concerts, friendships, the media, correspondence etc.

A. A Family Setting

A small group from the church, with the guidance of the pastor, can arrange in advance to visit them -- as a family. Ask them to invite their immediate family members, say grand parents or children, whichever applies. The date and time must be most convenient for them. This special setting brings Christ through family prayers and witnessing. As usual, prior to all this, prepare yourself by praying for the family. If you know them by name, do pray for them by name. Prepare a short sermon, familiar hymns and choruses. A testimony or two is proper. Mind you, this is not a private thing, but a family worship service. It is all right for neighbours to know that there is a prayer meeting, although it is not wise to invite them.

Generally the following may be your order of worship in the home:
1. Warm, friendly meeting and greetings, self-introductions -- naming your pastor and church. Be sure to clearly say you are sent by Jesus Christ, not by the church. This makes a special impact on them.
2. Then say: "We have come to share Jesus Christ with you. But do you have any concerns that we can pray together? Are there any problems you are facing as a family? Are there any joys that you would like to thank God for, the Giver of all good things? (Give time for this process).
3. Then pray for each of the concerns and joys mentioned, one by one. Making each of them special.
4. Ask if they know songs they have heard somewhere which they like, so you can sing together with them. Get them to participate, not to be spectators.

5. Bring your own songs and chorus which specifically focus on your evangelistic agenda.
6. Share your testimonies -- what Jesus has done for you, and your families. Avoid giving the impression that you are better than they are. Do not despise them. Choose your words carefully in preparing your testimony. Standard Scriptures for occasions like this are: John 3:16-17; Luke 15:11-24; Matt. 3:12-17; Matt. 16:24-27; Eph. 6:1-4 etc.
7. Appeal to them to accept Jesus Christ. If they seem reluctant or outright refuse, do not argue but quickly, close the service by prayer committing them to Christ so that He will continue to talk to them after you have departed. If they accept, write their names down.
8. Invite them to Church. If possible, promise to come get them.

Basically listen to the Holy Spirit because He is your invisible partner as is Christ, in evangelism. Please note, what works in the home may not work in other situations, say in a school setting.

B. School/Institutions

For all the troubles on the African continent, we are blessed in that most governments normally allow the teaching of Christianity in their schools. In fact, at the Ordinary and Advanced Levels of high school education examinations, Religious Knowledge is one of the more popular subjects. Schools are open to the preaching of the gospel. One can therefore approach heads of schools for (a) an opportunity to preach Christ possibly over a weekend, (b) a time once a week to conduct Christian worship with any size group, from two people to thousands. One just has to advertise so both the students and teachers know the venue and time for the event. You can write letters (like Paul writing to churches and individuals) and full-length sermons to be mailed out to students. The school administration may be willing to furnish students' addresses. In other words, most educational institutions are open to religious activities right on their campuses. Some events are ecumenical, while others are strictly denominational. My experience has been that numerous students have accepted Christ in such occasions. I am one of those who accepted Christ at an Easter revival at Old Mutare Mission at the age of 13. In fact, most of the young people who were involved in the liberation struggle in their respective countries in Africa are products of mission schools. Some of them are wonderful Christians and leaders in their respective denominations; others are waiting to be evangelised by you.

C. Weekday Evening Evangelism Meetings

In order to suite people who are busy with different occupations during the day, arrange a suitable venue, preferably a civic place, accessible to most people by private and public transportation. It has been observed that in some instances, non-church people feel better to be called to a neutral place than to some known sanctuary for religious meetings. They do not feel like they are strangers at neutral places. Also it is helpful to select a place that is prestigious so that the invitees feel drawn to it. Send the invitations to all residents in the target areas. Where people do not have postal services, send the youth to invite them by word of mouth or deliver written invitations.

The reason for holding these weeknight services, all week long, is to give an opportunity for those who may be totally prohibited by work commitments, during the day. Some may have other situations that make it hard, if not impossible, to attend daylight revivals. Although we expect regular attendance, if they miss one day, they can still attend another without missing the whole purpose. Mind you, this is a fishing "revival" meeting. You will have some churchgoers who need reviving just as badly as the non-Christians who may be interested in the Christian faith.

This type of evangelistic service must be dominated with powerful singing. Elsewhere in this book I have pointed out that in love and charity, without implying a "holier than thou" attitude, people may call gatherings "REVIVALS" when in fact the spirit which revives is completely absent. So these revivals have to be prepared and prayed for. We have already discussed the importance of prayer in the previous chapters.

D. A Day's Community Concert

The purpose of this gathering is to attempt to draw people who do not go to any church. In what appears to be secular environment, the gospel can still be preached and people can be converted because the Holy Spirit moves in mysterious ways. Furthermore, no invitees feel like strangers because everybody is a "visitor" at this public place. Also, since the concert is free for all, invite the whole community. Be sure to include community leaders, chiefs, political party leaders and church leaders as well as the rank and file. If you can serve some refreshments, do so. Give special recognition to any prominent members present. Blessed and challenged with a captive audience, the evangelist must present an interesting program. For instance, open the event with first class evangelistic singing followed by a first class brief evangelistic sermon before turning the time to the Director of Ceremonies [not Master of Ceremonies].

Experience has showed us that *that* short period of time does make a Christian impact on all present. As the rest of the events unfold, leave the Holy Spirit to do His work through the Scriptures, the sermon, the singing, the social and spiritual interaction and in spite of these. The opening devotion at such occasions should not exceed 30 minutes. Days later, this 30-minute long devotion may be followed by strategies such as tactfully visiting each of the invitees who showed interest in Christianity. Those who already belong to some churches will be refuelled spiritually; the unchurched may begin to show interest in Christ. But as an evangelist you have done your part to invite people to Christ. Also follow up different categories of leaders with a personal visit or a letter to invite them to church.

E. Through Friendships

In every community there are some people who are connected to others through friendships. Evangelism can take advantage of the network, but we can also utilise situations where those who do not have friends are glad to "make friends" with the purpose of evangelising.

Making friends with the lonely is a discreet strategy. Do all you can to create friendships with prospective converts. This Christian evangelistic courtship of friends has been used to create the right atmosphere within which people are invited to Christ. Make friends with a Holy sub-intention of winning them for Christ after a while. Some people have actually married unchurched spouses who eventually accepted Christ. This is also what happens when, say a Christian marries a Muslim or vice-versa. The point here being that marriage has been known to be a context within which people convert. It is a slow process, but with patience, a lot of prayer and persistence, it will eventually pay dividends when you finally invite your friend to be a Christian and even join the church. Prior to such friendship you may have exchanged visits in each other's homes, exchanged gifts like good friends usually do. This method of winning people to Christ is especially applicable in cultures that are not open to "strangers" calling on their door to talk about Jesus -- that capitalize on "privacy" and "individualism". But in Zimbabwe strangers may knock on the door. In fact when there is a knock on the door, the resident is expected to be hospitable.

F. Crusade: Harvesting Masses

In prior chapters, we have discussed how our Lord Jesus used personal evangelism with great success! He was also motivated to evangelise at the site of the masses: ".... when He saw the crowd, He went up on a mountainside...He began to teach them" [Matt. 5:1-2]. Although we do not have the actual numbers, it must have been a large gathering, which moved Jesus to deliver the famous and piercing sermon on the mountain.

We have discussed evangelising at funerals and weddings and how you just have to be prepared to act and improvise. Often there is no time for any meaningful planning. Crusades are different because their purpose is designed for a targeted harvest of souls. As usual, the event is planned months in advance so every possible detail can be taken care of to favour success because preaching to the masses is like people fishing with nets -- they expect to catch thousands at one time.

This method of evangelising has been used for ages by roving evangelists. It has its drawbacks but since this method is practiced universally, here I simply wish to remind those who embark on it to remember certain non-negotiable aspects.

1. Hark to the invitation which comes through the Holy Spirit.

> "During the night Paul had a vision of a man of Macedonia standing and begging him, 'come over to Macedonia and help us.' After Paul had seen the vision, we got ready at once to leave for

Macedonia, concluding that God had called us to preach the gospel to them" (Acts 16:9-10).

So in planning a crusade, ask yourself: where does God want me to run the crusade? God will certainly give you guidance. The key is to pray for the entire event. Pray before the event, everyday of the event, during each session of the crusade until the day the final benediction is pronounced. Pray for the community authorities, the venue, your staff, the message and especially for the Holy Spirit to take charge. Pray for obedience to the Holy Spirit.

2. Make adequate preparation. Advertise sufficiently, through the public, radio, TV, newspapers, pamphlets, persons, letters including the venue, date and time.
3. Train the volunteers how to minister at the altar during altar calls. Also give orientation to those assisting the evangelist, other ministers and counsellors.
4. Select the most talented preachers to assist the main preacher during the crusade, hoping that the main preacher is one of the most talented evangelistic preachers available.
5. There should be special music, powerful gospel singers. Remember singers preach through music, which should start at the very opening of each service. In fact the music should "tell " people it is time to begin. Sing the most popular and heart moving hymns.
6. After singing one or two moving songs, allow one or two testimonies especially suitable for the occasion -- typically, a testimony on how someone got salvation, a testimony of how Jesus transforms life is ideal.
7. Draw the net -- the altar call[16].
8. Establish a record of the converts. Refer them to the denomination of their choice, if they have any. For those who don't, make suggestions. They will need a home church.

One serious weakness of this method is that often some evangelists neglect to follow-up new converts with in-depth Christian education. From what I hear,

---

[16] Even though some have their reservation about invitational system, I find it has merit. Indeed it came only fairly recently in the history of the Christian faith and some say even John Wesley may never have heard, let alone used it. I find it has the advantage of causing a convert to physically move from one place to another -- from his/her seat to the altar. This is psychologically symbolic of leaving behind one way of existence (the discomfort of sin) and walking towards a new life -- salvation or new birth. The other advantage is for a person to make a public display of their decision which they will not repudiate easily. I suppose the natural extension of this perspective is that, if possible, when the converts leave the altar, they must then not return to the same seat/s they were sitting in before the altar call. This completes the symbolism as though to say, "I am moving on." I leave this for you to ponder and decide. The point is you should draw-in the net.

its worst critics call it a "hit and run" sort of thing. The evangelist comes, preaches, people get converted or revitalised and after the crusade, they go back home without further spiritual guidance, not to mention pastoral care. Like newly born babies who do not have milk and other suitable food to feed on, they eventually die. Those who are reborn at the spiritual revivals generally need spiritual feeding normally provided by the Church. In spite of this weakness, evangelists deserve credit for the initial step to invite non-believers to Christ. Nothing is more important than bringing lost souls to the Lord of the Harvest. I have reiterated elsewhere in this book that a religious meeting is not necessarily a "revival ". It can turn out to be just a social function, a well-organised gathering without producing any spiritual results. It becomes a revival when God has answered a lot of prayer of faith and resulting in persons being converted or spiritually revitalized. Therefore, there must be serious prayer for the presence of the Holy Spirit before and while the crusade is in progress.

G. Media: Radio-Television

Mass evangelism can also be achieved through the use of the various forms of mass media -- the electronic media is especially effective and popular i.e. radio and TV. It can reach anybody within the radius of the radio band. Radio is especially effective because it reaches people even if they are not aware that they are hearing the gospel. Buy airtime and especially when you can present the gospel through music, preaching and counselling to the world out there as far as the network can carry your message. Be sure to include a physical and postal/mailing address, telephone number and website where persons who accept Christ through the TV or radio program can write back so that they arrange for a church of their choice. Evangelists are faithful to the Lord. They know they can not pastor effectively electronically; so they let people join the denomination of their choice after conversion.

H. Letters and Messengers [in native languages]

A congregation can secure names, addresses and e-mail addresses through relatives of those who are too far from home to reach by teams of two; this includes family members who are overseas. If your family member is in the Diaspora for example, would they not benefit from an invitation to accept Christ -- in their native language. Such an invitation from home could change their life -- Holy Spirit willing. Thank God technology has made evangelism easier, but we still must pray for all our efforts to evangelise. Evangelism by mail is no less a work of faith. For example, all the names and letters are brought to the altar for prayer. Different people will pray and let the leader/pastor close the session by offering a prayer for each name.

Here is a sample letter:

Dear Mr and Mrs Tagashiratenzi, [We have received Christ.]

We hope you are well and in good health. We want you to know that because you were created in God's image, God loves you and cares for you day and night wherever you are. And, God has sent us through His Holy Spirit to ask you to give your life to Jesus Christ - now. Mr. or Mrs. Tagashiratenzi just repeat these words and from the bottom of your heart:

God, my heavenly father, I give my life to you now. I want to follow you from now on for the rest of my life. Please forgive me of all my sins and for not following your law. I now open my heart and my life to you. I now accept the words of the Bible which say 'If we confess our sins, He [Jesus] is faithful and just and will forgive us our sins, and purify us from all unrighteousness.' But 'if we claim we have not sinned, we make him (Jesus) out to be a liar [1 John 1:9-10]. Thank you Jesus for forgiving me. I now belong to you. I pray this in the name of Jesus Christ. Amen.

Then from this hour on, just believe that you have been forgiven, and you are now a Christian. Halleluiah! Amen!

We are yours, sent to you by Jesus Christ.

Names:.. ....
Pastor's Name: ....
Name of your Church: ....
Address:..
Telephone #:...
Email: ....

Seven
THE PASTOR IS KEY

I. CASES IN POINT

Jesus' words to Peter clearly indicate that the shepherd is the key to the nourishment of the congregation.

> *When they had finished eating, Jesus said to Simon Peter, Simon son of John, "Do you truly love me more than these?" "Yes, Lord... you know that I love you...." Said Peter. Jesus said, "Feed my lambs" (John 21:15) ... and again... "feed my sheep" (John 21:17).*

In this final chapter we consider evangelism as not only winning new souls but also feeding those who are already churched. The congregation needs to be continuously spiritually nourished in order to grow strong to maturity and in service. They need a shepherd who himself or herself is spiritually connected to the chief Shepherd, Jesus Christ, and is sacrificially committed to service.

It is my strongest conviction that the pastor is key to the success or failure of the ministry at the local church. The congregation will thrive if it is fed well on the Word. The pastor plays a major role that determines whether the congregation is healthy or sickly; whether the congregation is characterized with spiritual vitality or spiritual coldness and weakness. The congregation can either be like the Dead Sea that does not have any life in it or like the Nile River which contributes to the life and prosperity wherever it reaches. In a nutshell, the pastor's responsibility is to ensure his congregation's salvation through his own. Let me explain.

During my 24 years as Episcopal leader of the United Methodist Church of the Zimbabwe Area, I arrived at a firm conclusion that the life and death of any congregation depends on the pastor. YES! I discovered that if a charge or a parish of more than one congregation was weak, sickly, unhealthy, inactive and almost lifeless, spiritually speaking, (usually signified by poor giving and attendance,) in most cases, the major problem was the leadership. If a new pastor was appointed to the same parish, the new personnel could bring dynamic change. When the new appointment was the only variant, it became apparent that the outgoing pastor had been the stumbling block. People started to come back to their home church because word went around that things were happening, new members joined, giving and tithing increased dramatically. The local churches resumed paying their assessments in full and in a timely fashion. Simply put there was new life. By the way, the phenomenon I have just described was observed in several other situations and repeatedly. In other words, it was not an isolated incident. Many preachers will not like this, but it is true. And since it is true, we should declare the truth from the top of the highest mountain peak in the whole world.

If we take this observation one step further, we find that the reverse is also true. It also worked out that a certain pastor would be appointed to a parish that is in good, healthy condition and it eventually became unhealthy, weak and poor. These observations are sufficient for us to draw a very critical conclusion about the vitality of a church and its evangelism -- the Pastor is Key. Consider the case of the Greendale UMC and Seke Central in Harare, Zimbabwe.

The Case of Greendale United Methodist Church

In Zimbabwe from April to August of each year, is the time for the annual Harvest Thanksgiving drive and celebration. The word of God tells us to: *"celebrate the feast of Harvest with the first fruits of the crops you sow in your fields. Celebrate the feast of ingathering at the end of the year, when you gather in your crops from the field" [Ex. 23:16].* Indeed, stewardship doctrine presents the United Methodists with a challenging and exciting season annually. Individuals, families, sections, local churches, circuits and districts offer money, crops, vegetables and livestock to God, their Creator and Provider. The operative concept here is "Thanksgiving to God."

Now let us examine the figures and giving pattern at Greendale United Methodist Church (UMC). In the year 2003, Greendale UMC raised Z$ 2 790 305.00 or USD450.00 for their annual Harvest Thanksgiving drive. This was really below average compared to its counterparts. A ready and conveniently plausible explanation is the demographics: Greendale UMC in Harare, the nation's capital, is located in a middle-income, low density neighbourhood. At the time of these figures, it had only been in existence a few years and they were engaged in the early stages of building a sanctuary and the pastor's office block. This may explain the below average statistics. Right?

No! No matter how plausible this sounds, it is totally unfounded. Here is the proof.

By 2004, under the new and dynamic leadership of Rev. Sanda Sanganza, that same congregation gave Z$ 51 202 210.00 or USD 8258.00. What makes this scenario strong evidence that the pastor is key is the fact that Rev. Sanganza took up this charge from January 2004 and, as we have already pointed out, Harvest Thanksgiving period ends in August. So in just under seven months of new leadership, the church broke its own record and beat its target many times over. The building project was still in progress. The cost of building material had quadrupled due to inflation. Ironically, the new pastor was only part-time, whereas his predecessor was full time!

Table 1: Greendale United Methodist Church Growth

Descriptions	2003	2004	Growth %age
Tithers	31	48	55 %
Tithers (Amount Paid)	USD 429 or Z$ 2 661 117	USD 5244 or Z$ 32 510 345	1122 %
Harvest Thanksgiving	USD 450.00 or Z$ 2 790 305	USD 8258 or Z$ 51 202 210	1735 %
Mission	USD 6 or Z$ 38 790	USD 319 or Z$ 1 977 475	4997 %
Membership	147	260	77 %
Church Attendance	104	154	48 %

Currency Exchange rate 1USD=Z$ 6200.00

We can also observe the following at this circuit.
- Sunday offering growth on average: 1400%
- 10% of all undesignated funds are now channelled in Missions' Works as of 2004.
- Since Greendale UMC started there was no Mission statement until February 2004.
- Leaders are more united/working as a team.

The Case of the Nyagato Clergy Couple: [A typology]

Through Bishop Christopher Jakomo's leadership, the United Methodist Church in Zimbabwe made the decision that the best way to support the work of our Lord Jesus is by *tithing*. Tithing is a biblical practice that most Christians tend to conveniently overlook. With the outstanding, committed leadership of a Holy Spirit filled pastor, Rev. Marcus Nyagato, Seke Central Circuit of the United Methodist Church in Chitungwiza, reached the highest percentage of tithers in the whole Zimbabwe Area -- 95%. In considering this achievement, it is important to note that this congregation is not in the capital city; it is located in a high density area where incomes are low. The pastor's spouse, Rev. Faith Nyagato, is a 'fiery' preacher and musician. She has brought the highest number of new persons to Christ -- a record in the ministry for the two Conferences in Zimbabwe. The Nyagatos are a special middle aged couple with five children and two grandchildren at the time of writing. They apparently find time to do the best for their Master, Jesus in spite of the daily struggle to fend for their family.

The Pastor is the Key -- in matters of spiritual vitality, stewardship, tithing or making disciples. Therefore, we have decided to devote this chapter to "The Pastor." Our purpose and hope is to encourage, not to discourage, this central figure as he or she goes about in ministry (in general) and evangelism (in particular).

II. WHERE DID WE GO WRONG

I have the strongest belief that the membership decline of some mainline denominations is primarily due to a spiritual lukewarm syndrome, or even a sort of spiritual coma they are experiencing. Let us look at the reasons behind this and how to run a diagnostic check on our person and congregation to determine whether or not we are on track in the King's business – God..

In my view, the problem can be traced back to "DOAFS" pastors/preachers[17], who somehow get appointments into the service of the Lord in spite of their infectious state. They step out into service without a benchmark for their own Christian Experience -- they have no personal relationship with God. I have no idea how they slip through but perhaps it has something to do with the often pointed out observation that most seminaries, I hear, have become spiritual cemeteries where both the professors and seminarians lack the spiritual vitality necessary for effective evangelism. The church has become only a maintenance organisation, rather than a resource for spirituality.

My very first trip to the United States of America was in August 1958. I have since returned many times and visited some 45 states of that country. I have been blessed to worship in at least a hundred churches. I have found it to be true that churches that are spiritually vibrant have pastors who are spirit-filled graduates of certain seminaries. In most cases, such seminaries still emphasize what the Bible teaches about salvation; firm belief in Jesus Christ, experience of the power of the Holy Spirit and the power of prayer in the life of the believer. You can call them "conservative", even "fundamentalists"; you may call them whatever you want, but the indisputable fact of the matter is that *preaching that is devoid of the Holy Spirit and emphasis on the power of Jesus Christ (who is Lord of the Church), is merely emotion arousing speaking, but not an evangelistic message.*

Major denominations, whether in Africa or in the West, which are declining seem NOT to realize that *the spirit makes the church grow* and that, *the pastor is key*. Most of them receive reports of membership decline every time they gather to reflect on the ministry. They blame this decline on social factors, the economy, on shifting demographics in surrounding neighbourhoods; but they fail, neglect or refuse to face the core cause head-on. There are statistics to substantiate this reality in your church records if you care to check. You will find the Greendale UMC case experience applies to you too.

It is ironic that in the United States, there is no religious persecution, and yet there is a serious concern about membership decline in the mainline denominations. So one cannot blame the decline on persecution. Don McGavran writes about how our future generations will look back on these days of

---

[17] A pastor who is "Dead on arrival from seminary".

declining membership and he observed that:

> "*All this took place in a free country, no church was being persecuted, seminaries were never freer, national prosperity was at an all-time high...institutions of learning attracted students from every nation on the face of the earth...public health stood at an all time high. Men and women were living longer lives; the rate of infant mortality had sharply declined. The battle of brotherhood was being won. Blacks were being treated more and more as fellow citizens rather than as members of an inferior race" (McGavran, 1988, 24).*

And yet, despite all these victories, we lost the battle of evangelising just because we did not read the signs.

This spiritual sickness symbolized by membership decline makes my heart sink. I am sure that I am not the only one who is concerned about the situation. Millions of other people bleed with shock, embarrassment, sadness and disappointment to see the church decline at a time in history when every advantage is stacked in our favour. Apparently something went wrong in our Christian disciple-making process, causing the present decline. Now the question is: what are we doing about it? What does common sense dictate? Let us first share an incident that demonstrates my point here.

Like those of you who have grandchildren, you have many stories about them. I have nine grandchildren. I will never forget what my granddaughter, Tenderano, told her father, Tanyaradzwa (Tanya), regarding his old car that gave him problems most of the time. She was four years old at the time. One day the car stalled right in the middle of the nation's capitol during rush hour traffic, causing not only inconvenience but also embarrassment. Impatient at being late for nursery school <u>again</u>, she had had enough of it, so she just looked at her father intensely and blurted out. "Daddy, why don't you get a new car?" The father tried to defend himself to comfort the daughter by saying "I don't have money to buy a better car ." She retorted, "First you need the brains to see that your car is rotten, then you need money. I saw you the other day depositing some money in the bank." It could have been a few hundred dollars she saw. Certainly it was not even enough to make a down payment on a new car. The point here is that the daughter appealed to "common sense."

As leaders of major denominations, don't we have the common sense to know that we are spiritually descending into the deep, deep pit of spiritual bankruptcy, due to scepticism, externalism and self-righteousness? Jesus detested all of these attitudes (Matt. 23:1-36). Don't we have the common sense to know that modernism, ultra liberalism, self-actualisation, self absorption have stricken us with spiritual hostility? We are spiritually hostile when we don't pay our prophets for preaching what needs to be said in the pulpit. This is similar to stoning our prophets. What we want to hear from our pulpits may not be what God is saying to us. Some of us have spiritual hostility about things that are very Biblical e.g. some now take the words, "Hallelujah" and "Amen" as if they are dirty words in our worship services (Rev. 22:20). Hallelujah simply expresses praise to God. To argue that shouting "Hallelujah" disturbs the faith is NOT consistent with the Scriptures: "Make a joyful noise to the Lord...." (Psalm 47:1, 66:1).

Don't we have the common sense to realize that Table 2 (below), spells and reveals to us that those who still preach the foundational doctrines such as sin, Christ, salvation, forgiveness, new birth, the Holy Spirit and the great commission are the ones with the increasing membership and are ahead of us in winning people? Yet generally, the mainline denomination congregations are facing a serious decline. It seems clear to me that our continued healthy existence is in jeopardy. We are "sick" while in the meantime the Pentecostal churches, which are spiritually vital, are booming. Think about it: we all use the same Bible -- the revealed Word of God -- and yet they flourish while our churches decline, even if we are located right next door to each other.

Table 2: World Church Growth Rates

Pentecostals	8.1 %
Evangelicals	5.4 %
All Protestants	3.3 %
Roman Catholics	1.3 %

Source: http://www.adherents.com/Religions_By_Adherents.html
(Last modified 6th September 2002)

Signs of a weak, unhealthy Congregation.

In the previous Chapter, I explained that sometimes people need to be told that they are in need of salvation. The facts may be staring them in the face but at times people somehow just don't get the message until it is spelled out to them. The same seems to apply to some congregations and denominations.

I believe that congregations, like human beings, have a personality -- good or bad; like an organism, they either get sick, or are strong and healthy; and they have vital signs that we can read, just as a doctor can read your blood-sugar level or blood pressure. Fortunately they can also be cured, if they are not well. In this section, let us think together about some of the common signs and symptoms of what I call A.D.C. -- Acute Distressed Congregation. Assuming that the reader belongs to some congregation, in this instance you can be your own physician, examine yourself and find out what kind of a church you are. We suggest you watch for the following symptoms although there may be more than these few:

➢ **No Mission Statement**:
A sick blind church does not have a mission statement. It does not know what it exists for. It operates and moves like a *zongororo* (millipede) -- groping in an imaginary darkness while the world is in full sunlight. What justification can there be for a congregation, that ought to be the

light of the world, to be in darkness?

- **Narcissism**:
  It does not have an evangelistic or an outreach program. It is quite ignorant about its task as a church. Wittingly or unwittingly it lives in defiance of Jesus' command to bring others to Christ. If it has any vision at all, then it is something myopic like, "our parish is our world." This is the exact reverse of John Wesley's global vision: *"The world is my parish."* Needless to say there is no budget for missions or evangelism.

- **Dwindling Membership**:
  It loses members. They go to other churches, other denominations or simply go nowhere. It is a membership killer. Members are starved to death i.e. by lack of spiritual feeding that should be provided by teaching and preaching. No new members ever join, year-in and year-out, not at Christmas, nor at Easter.

- **Unspiritual**:
  It does not take prayer seriously. The congregation is quite ignorant about the importance and power of prayer in a person's life and in the life of the church. In addition to killing membership, it also destroys the spirituality in members who have not left yet. Either the congregation is unaware of the fact that Jesus took prayer very seriously or they are just too materialistic and lazy.

- **No Bible Study**:
  A church that does not hold regular Bible classes during the week or even on Sunday is unhealthy. It will not remain "sick" indefinitely. It will eventually die, at least spiritually.

- **Poor Finances**:
  The congregation fails to meet its budgeted giving to God, whom they worship. Their understanding of Stewardship is materialistic, not spiritual.

- **No Team Spirit**:
  It is characterised with internal friction. The spirit of Jesus' love, peace, unity and mutual forgiveness does not rule the hearts of the members, nor the leadership. They thrive on gossip, rather than the gospel.

- **No Holy Spirit**:
  The pulpit might be equipped with everything, except the power of the Holy Spirit. The pulpit is just a podium, not Mt. Calvary from which grace pours. Everything is ice-cold.

- **Resistance To Change**:
  The congregation does not like change. It is like the children of Israel who, when confronted with challenges, would complain to Moses: "... was it because there were no graves in Egypt that you brought us to the desert to die?" (Ex. 14:11). The congregation's favourite responses to change is: " We have always done it this way ." -- which is why they have always been dying!

> **Cold To Visitors**:
> It does not like strangers. It resents visitors; worse still if a stranger is of a different race, poor or elderly! This is the home of intolerance. Everyone owns an earmarked pew and woe unto anyone who sits in "my pew." It is as though certain seats have an invisible sign which reads, "Reserved for X".

> **Lifelessness**:
> Attendance is poor in numbers and it is erratic i.e. members don't attend regularly. Those who do attend, lack the vigour that is normally associated with God's children. There is no church choir to sing and enrich the worship service. People sing hymns through their mouths but not from their hearts. There is no youth group, no women's group, no men's group and no fellowship between members and their families. Children have to be forced to go to church on Sunday morning. Nothing new happens from one week to the next. It may as well have a nickname, St. Pathetic Congregation.

> **Wrong Concept Of Church**:
> Quite wrongly and ignorantly they say, "Visiting the sick, shut-ins, and the elderly is the pastor's business. That's what he is paid to do." Quite wrong! If the early church had taken this kind of attitude and taken the position that it was the business of only the twelve disciples to evangelise, the gospel would have taken a long, long time to reach us. They don't seem to appreciate that Jesus sent more than just *the twelve* to witness (Luke 10:1-3).

Is any of this sounding familiar to you? Is this describing someone or a congregation you know? Now someone may say: "So what if the congregation is 'sick' and is 'dying'?" Some may not even care to revive the congregation. I must remind everyone that it is our Christian duty to reinstate *St. Pathetic* just as when Jesus was reinstating Peter after his fall by denying him; one of the instructions He gave was that if you love me "Feed my lambs" (John 21:16). We have a duty to pass on this church (in good health) and the gospel. Every effort must be made to see that the youth grows with Christ and nurtured by the Church so that they may grow as Jesus did: "And Jesus grew in wisdom and stature, and in favour with God and (people)" (Luke 2:52). If we do not take up this noble task, I am afraid the devil will; and he will do so without any competition or challenge.

III. RESURRECTING A DYING CONGREGATION

The next section discusses our humble suggestions that may help resurrect a distressed congregation. Unfortunately, this may require a change of pastoral leadership to give the congregation "a new start." The reason we say "unfortunately" is because it does not necessarily mean the only way to regain a congregation's vitality is by changing leaders. It is a sad statement about any pastor when they move-on because they can not capture the essence and urgency for their own change in order to facilitate restoration of the church to its intended path. We want to believe that any pastor who is in full spiritual contact with his/her boss, God, must be capable of self examination to reach the conclusion that they themselves need to change first in order for them to restore a church and its members to vitality. However, indeed one way or the other, the pastoral leadership must be transformed before they can be a useful key to congregational turn around.

For a new pastor at a church, revitalizing a weak, sickly and unhealthy congregation involves a careful self-examination by the entire congregation, especially current church leadership, guided by the new pastor. Ideally a new pastor normally has the requisite objectivity to diagnose the new congregation and hopefully implement the measures to revitalize it. Here we simply suggest some traditional corrective measures:

A. Core Group:

The Pastor needs, first and foremost, to identify spiritually vivacious members of the congregation. There may be as few as just two or three members who form an essential core (Matt. 18:20). Organise them into a prayer group that convenes regularly in obedience to the Holy Spirit. Of course the pastor would have to be part of this core group. Meet two or three times a week for prayer in general, and in particular, pray for the Holy Spirit to revive your church. Pray for the pastor and the lay leader. Pray that the Holy Spirit ousts the demons of self-righteousness, spiritual emptiness, a holier than thou and all judgemental attitudes. Pray for the anointing of your church by the Holy Spirit. The Zimbabwe people are fortunate because the Holy Spirit (the Pentecost experience) once visited them in 1918 at Old Mutare Mission in a big way. Remember this happened after a lot of praying. This 1918 Zimbabwe Pentecost can recur when God wants to. But pray for God's presence which is actually your openness to divine presence. Do not be shy to call upon God's Holy Spirit. Yes, name Him. Pray for the revival of your church. Cry to God: "revive us again here at St Pathetic." Jesus says, "if you believe, you will receive whatever you ask for in prayer" (Matt. 21:22). Pray until the Lord answers your prayer. The group may become larger as you go along. That is part of the answer to prayer. When this happens, it is important to remain humble and be grateful to God.

B. Mission:

A church that decides on and develops a mission outreach will find itself growing because members tend to develop a sense of obedience to God. When you reach out you get life fulfilment. But if you say: "The congregation is our world, " the result is lifelessness. The core group must share their vision with the few members who are regular attendees. It is recommended that the group set a realizable goal.

C. Inclusiveness:

Human beings need to feel important. To keep everyone active, try to assign people to various taskforces within the congregation. The practice of overburdening one person with duties, while other members who are equally capable do nothing, should be discouraged because it is not productive.

D. Bible Study:

The Word of God, the Bible, has a wonderful way of speaking to people, changing their attitudes and negative life styles. It makes Christians grow in spiritual maturity. Therefore, organise your entire church into study groups. Assign a capable group leader, to guide Bible study, otherwise the Pastor must lead. All attendees must be encouraged to own Bibles and not only that, they should be encouraged to study them.

E. Training "Disciples":

Identify members for training to go out in twos to evangelise personally (Luke 10:1-3). In Chapter Six, we discussed at length the quality, power, effectiveness and fruitfulness of personal evangelism using the face-to-face approach. We shall not dwell on it here. Suffice to say it generally produces amazing results for the congregation. If you train the volunteers and encourage many to go out to witness, you will be surprised how much they actually enjoy doing it. Furthermore they even grow strong in their own Christian faith. Regarding evangelism, we agree that "...evangelism is not an option. It is an imperative, and we had better be about the task " (Armstrong 1979. 13). This is not just for the pastor, either. It is a task for all Christians, the entire congregation. "Without evangelism, no one becomes a committed Christian, and without evangelism, no one continues to grow into vital Christian maturity. If this task is not done, the Christian community cannot exist; if it is not done continuously in the Christian community, it may soon degenerate into formal religious institution" (Job 1970.23).

F. Lively Worship Service:

Create lively, contagious services. First it is quite important to agree to the time of worship service, which should be convenient, and relaxed, so people do not feel inconvenienced or rushed. For example, in Zimbabwe, we used to have church services at 2:00 p.m., but with time, it became necessary to change the tradition to having services in the morning because there were soccer matches, which attracted numerous potential worshippers in the afternoons. The worship service must be interesting and meaningful -- a time to communion with God. Through reading the Scriptures, prayers, creeds, music -- whether solos, special music or the choir or congregational singing -- worshippers must feel at home, touched and moved. Then all is climaxed by a good inspirational and challenging sermon. Anything a worshipper sees, hears, and feels, affects a sense of closeness to God.

In Africa, the drum is a traditional instrument, which has been used only to announce either danger, war, death, or birth celebration and to evoke dancing. It is now also used to stimulate a moving worship experience. Worshippers who feel like dancing are encouraged to do so, all to the glory of God. Other cultures use the organ or piano for the same effect. Hymns or choruses sung to traditional tunes but with gospel lyrics tend to invoke intense spirituality. The denominations which are experiencing population decline may want to try contemporary worship services because it is a step in the right direction. There is a cry for relevance in worship. In this regard, I agree with Terry Madison's observation that, "worship in African American churches is joyful and celebrative. Worshippers interact with the preacher and music. The services are typically spontaneous.... The worshippers' warm enthusiasm is complemented by powerful preaching" (Madison 2002, 152). If a worship service is conducted effectively it should inspire the worshipper to live a Christ-like life throughout the coming week, at least. Furthermore, the worshipper feels a deep desire to come back the following Sunday. By word of mouth, typically worshippers will invite their friends to "come and see" (John 4:29), for themselves.

G. Create Fellowship Activities:

Have creative fellowship activities during the week, not just on Sunday. Remember one of the values of religion is a sense of belonging, fellowship -- as the early churches did. "They devoted themselves to the Apostles' teaching and to the fellowship, to the breaking of bread and to prayer" (Acts 2:42), when the Christian community started, we are told. Many people do not realize that fellowship, whether it is composed of two or a crowd, is therapeutic for the soul. Organising such a fellowship satisfies the religious, psychological and physical needs of worshippers. Good fellowship can be a mini-worship service, yet very meaningful. A group of Christians may gather for games, prayer, song, speeches, poems, food, special music, choir practice or whatever reason and end up praising God, no matter how informal the setting. Because they enjoy the fellowship, they will want to repeat such gatherings over and over.

H. Invite Spirit-Filled Speakers:

It is advisable to invite talented speakers every time a guest is called -- now and again. Some preachers are reluctant to invite guest preachers due to jealousy; guests can revitalise the congregation. Feeling jealous? Clearly, a prayerful pastor who realizes that she or he is key to church revitalization will have to pray: "get behind me, Satan, you are a stumbling block to me..." (Matt. 16:23). We noted earlier that one of the symptoms of a dying church is narcissism. The remedy is preaching, inviting guests, allowing the Holy Spirit to move you where He may, for the sake of the salvation and spiritual vitality of the many souls. It is to Gods' glory and your praise when the congregation has come to life.

I. Organise Choirs:
We suggest you organise a good powerful choir, a soul-moving choir, including youth and children's choirs. Remember that choirs assist the preacher every Sunday. They, like the preacher, bring the gospel but through music. The church Administration Board must provide the choir with all it needs to preach through music. Choir robes generally make the choir distinct and attractive.

J. Encourage Testimonies:
Encourage your members to give testimonies during the church services, if they want to. Sharing what God has done is a powerful way of revitalising weak members because they begin to realize that God is doing His thing

-- the old time religion is still good enough! However, such testimonies must be "screened " to encourage rather than discourage others.

K. Spiritual Revival:
Organise evangelistic meetings and pray that they may turn out to be true "revivals", not just a secular gathering under the guise of a revival. Once again I want to remind you that not all revival meetings will necessarily "revive" the spirit. But evangelistic meetings may and can turn out to be real revivals only if you pray for that to happen, long before the meeting takes place.

There are various methods: either organise such meetings for the entire congregation for one week, evenings only or weekends only; or even one full day can be used with at least three to four services the same day. The pastor may choose to organise a revival for a special group: women, men, youth, with special emphasis on that target group.

You may even organise evangelistic meetings in homes. Zimbabwean United Methodists have discovered real power in having what they call "section meetings". These are groups organised according to the geographic location surrounding the local church. One may say this is a new version of the "class meetings " of John Wesley's time in England. They are run like a mini church congregation, with prayer, testimonies, preaching, eating together, Bible study, singing, and collecting the offering for the Harvest Thanksgiving. Typically the meetings are led by trained laity. Some groups/sections work hard to win new members. They can invite the pastor or a guest preacher for evangelistic preaching at their section meeting. Spiritual disciplines: Prayer, Bible Study, worship, fellowship, meditation, fasting and witness can be practiced effectively in those groups. However, we do need to reiterate that what happens in sectional or congregational worship generally reflects the overall pastoral leadership.

IV. SIX TRAITS OF AN EVANGELISTIC PREACHER

God calls men and women to preach His word. Let us discuss some of the major characteristics of the one who would spearhead the revitalization of any congregation which would otherwise pack up and close its doors. In his book

How to Bring Men to Christ, Torrey says the preacher "must himself (sic) be a thoroughly converted person" (Torrey 1984, 7). *One must know the Jesus of experience. This is non negotiable.* God must have touched one somehow, somewhere at some time. God's preachers need genuine experience of the Lord, the kind Moses proclaimed following his encounter with God at the burning bush (Gen. 3:2-10). The same was true of Isaiah in the temple (Is. 6:6-7). Jeremiah also could say he was anointed by God (Jer. 1:4-9) after being moulded in his mother's womb by Him. Paul would say Jesus touched him on the road to Damascus (Acts 9:4-6) Peter would testify that on the Day of Pentecost (Acts 2:4) he was touched by the Lord. As for John Wesley, his power came from *the strange warming of the heart* caused by the Holy Spirit at Alders gate. Yes, indeed! I believe that by the time a minister receives Ministerial Orders, the Holy Spirit should have already "ordained" him or her. Of course the church still has to do its doctrinal and polity rituals, but let no one think that the laying on of hands on a ministerial candidate gives him or her what the Holy Spirit has not already assigned to the individual. This thinking was in part confirmed by one of my pastors in Zimbabwe Area -- Conrad Chigumira. There was "something" about Conrad that characterized him as the ideal evangelist.

A. Baptized in Holy Spirit: The Rev. Conrad Chigumira

The United Methodist Church in Zimbabwe Area will never ever be the same because a man by the name of Conrad Chigumira was used by the Holy Spirit enough to make a mark in the twentieth century history of Christianity in Zimbabwe. Rev. Chigumira was evidently a spirit-filled evangelist preacher, in deed.

In the early 1970s, the United Methodist Church in Zimbabwe decided to expand northward, westward, and southward[18]. Hearing the echoes of John Wesley, "The world is my parish", we even went beyond the national borders to Zambia, Malawi, Botswana and South Africa.

The Masvingo District of the United Methodist Church, covering the southern region of Zimbabwe, was almost single-handedly established by Pastor Conrad Chigumira. Churches and preaching points started mushrooming all over as a result of his spirit-filled preaching accompanied by miraculous healing, exorcisms and all. Demons were cast out in the name of Jesus; the sick were healed by faith; and the unchurched persons were converted through the power of the Holy Spirit. *In deed,* he was a spirit-filled preacher, the ideal pastor/evangelist. His work spoke for itself.

One day when he was visiting Chiredzi Hospital, Pastor Chigumira tells how he, by faith, helped a near fatal case of breached birth. The nurses were waiting

---

[18] To give a little background information: for a long time the United Methodist Church in Zimbabwe was confined to the east of the country as a result of the gentlemen's agreement among the first missionaries from England and those from the United States of America. After Zimbabwe's political independence, it became self-defeating to continue to honour such an unbiblical, unproductive, evangelism-unfriendly arrangement.

for a doctor to come from Mutare, 120 miles (193 kilometres) -- some two-and-half hours away, to perform a caesarean operation. Pastor Chigumira told the nurses that he could pray for the woman so she could deliver naturally. He says, of course they thought he was some crazy or foolish old man who did not understand the laws of nature. In spite of this, they decided they had nothing to lose by letting him pray; after all, they felt they were just being courteous to him, especially considering that the only thing the nurses could do was wait for the doctor to arrive! So he was allowed to pray for the woman who was in the valley of the shadow of death. Long before the doctor arrived, to the shattering amazement of the nurses, the woman delivered naturally. Pastor Chigumira's effectiveness as an evangelist/pastor was enhanced by such miracles as this, one after another, empowered by the promise in Matt. 10:1.

Such power as this characterizes an effective evangelist. Who was Conrad? A man about six feet tall, no seminary training, and no college degree -- just his "Damascus Road experiences". Like St. Paul or John Wesley, he repeatedly testified how lost he was before he accepted the Lord as his Saviour and allowed Him to rule his life. He used to parade his former wicked life publicly like Paul did. Though he was one of the least theologically educated pastors in our Conference, Rev. Chigumira's spiritual qualification was the best -- the Alders' gate-like experience. He was filled with the Holy Spirit and so he preached like Paul, prayed like Peter, sang like John, preached like only Chigumira could, evangelised like evangelism was intended and indeed he healed like the Lord Himself -- without anaesthesia. The power of the Holy Spirit equipped him to preach, pray and above all, heal by faith. Indeed he was a vessel of the Holy Spirit.

As Bishop, I was heavily criticised for letting a person with hardly any academic qualification join the ministry with the title "Reverend". But I had recognised and acknowledged that, spiritually speaking, he was the best qualified evangelist/pastor of the Word in the whole Conference because God had already *made him* by the time I, as the resident Bishop, formally ordained him. Yes, he surely was! Furthermore, Pastor Chigumira delivered the goods, which Jesus ordered us to, namely preaching repentance and effective disciple making. So effective was Pastor Chigumira that some people accepted Christ even at his funeral service; even in death, he was the consummate evangelist. I can think of no one better to illustrate what an evangelist should be -- Conrad, I salute you.

B.   Equipped with the Holy Spirit.

An evangelist must be filled with the Holy Spirit. Jesus promised " but you will receive power when the Holy Spirit comes on you: and you will be my witness..." (Acts 1:8). In the context of evangelism that decolonizes souls, a preacher without the Holy Spirit is like a bricklayer without mortar or like a carpenter without a hammer, a saw and a plane or a motor mechanic without a spanner. We have already discussed who the Holy Spirit is. So we simply argue that He is indispensable. The Holy Spirit is a pre-requisite for fruitful evangelism that decolonizes the soul.

C. A Person of the Bible.

The main purpose for the Bible is not scholarly consideration: it is meant to change lives of people so that they may also pick it up, read it and pass on the message. The time I spent studying in the Holy Land made me understand that indeed the Bible was written for a different culture from mine: like many other cultures, its people are just hanging on to their ways against outside influences. Therefore how can an African evangelist, for example, understand the cultural nuances in the Bible, when his own culture is under daily threat from forces that cloud his perceptions? Indeed a Bible study class may help but to read it prayerfully is the most productive way. Pray that God will reveal its meaning as you read it.

The Bible is the chief and most important book for effective evangelist because its authority validates the sermon. As the revealed Word, it conveys God's message to humanity. Hearers listen attentively to a sermon that is based on the Word of God. In order to effectively interpret the message to the congregation, an evangelist does not just need a Bible (the book); he/she also needs a sound grasp of its contents. Indeed the preacher needs to have surrendered to its commands. Effective preachers believe that the Bible is the revelation of God in print. It is both His love letter to us and a covenant with all creation. Therefore it must be treated with the highest regard and the importance it deserves. It is a compliment to the preacher if he or she is renown as one who is totally dependent on the Bible when he delivers. Know the Bible.

D. Monkey-see, Monkey-do.

The preacher must be of a respectable character and reputation; this personal integrity is crucial because you cannot effectively preach what you are not. Aristotle the philosopher once said, "What you are, speaks so loudly; I cannot hear what you say. What you seem to be to me, speaks so loudly that it influences my response to what you say" (Aristotle n.d. 76). So whether we like it or not, the response to our message, to some extent, is influenced by how we, the preachers, are perceived by the congregation. The message you deliver each Sunday is secondary to the message you convey all week long.

Having said this, we need to immediately caution the reader that pretence does not go very far. The saying is true that "you cannot fool all the people all the time". People usually can see through hypocrisy. In sum, *character or reputation gives integrity and power to the message.* I often hear people asked to pray for the preacher, when he or she is already in the pulpit, say: Lord let us not see, the human being in front of us, but You." This is a prayer to invoke the Holy Spirit, but at the same time, the prayer implies that if they [the worshippers] were to listen to the preacher as a human being, there would be little or nothing to learn. When I hear this, I often wonder if this is a veiled insult. I leave the reader to decide. Whichever way one looks at this pre-preaching prayer, the issue of integrity is a vital character trait in this calling.

E. Prayerful and Obedient

Prayerfulness is another major characteristic of an evangelistic preacher. He or she values prayer because it has tremendous power. *Prayer is power*. If prayer aims at bringing contact between God and the worshipper, it follows that prayer, like the Holy Spirit, is indispensable in the life of a preacher, if one desires to be a highly effective and fruitful spokesperson for God.

F. Christ Centred

A preacher who knows *the Jesus of experience* is always filled with the Holy Spirit. One without the Holy Spirit is like a brand new automobile without fuel. No matter how beautiful it may appear, it cannot have any "mobility." And so one may ask: of what use is it? To which St. Paul would answer: "Its like a clanging cymbal " (1 Corinthians 13:1).

A preacher who knows the Lord Jesus has a ravenous hunger to present Christ and win souls for Him; he has a deep desire for the salvation of the lost and will always preach and witness whenever a chance arises. This is why Paul said "Brothers, my heart's desire and prayer to God for the Israelites is that they may be saved " (Rom. 10:1). Just as the deep desire of a person who was truly called to be a physician is to heal patients so they live a healthy life, that of any committed school teacher is to give an education to the pupil, *the evangelistic preacher desires that all may accept Christ as their personal Lord and Saviour*. John Knox once said: "give me Scotland or I die." Knox was expressing a deep desire that his nation be saved. As a Methodist, and more importantly a disciple of Jesus Christ, I share John Wesley's vision that "the world is my parish," and my desire is that all may receive the Good News that Jesus is Lord. Such is the passion, *holy passion* which must characterize an effective evangelistic preacher.

V. PREPARATION OF AN EVANGELISTIC SERMON

To argue that 'The Pastor is Key' is a major position because he or she virtually controls the overall ministry of the church at the congregation's level. We believe it is a fair assessment based on our experience of parish life.

A. Inspiration

Any sermon worthy of the label must be inspired by God, but this is especially necessary if the sermon is to be an effective evangelistic one. The sermon must be from God who gives inspiration, discernment and vision. Therefore we must start preparing the sermon by asking God in prayer what it is He wants His people to hear through the preacher and in spite of the preacher. I believe that even when a committee assigns the topic for the guest preacher, it is God who inspires the committee and therefore God will provide you the content for that topic! If my reader were the pastor, I would ask you to imagine your congregation in front of you, with their *need* for hope, courage to face their fears, strength to resist temptations and fears caused by unknown diseases and all. The congregation stands before you in need of power to overcome various religious, social, political and transitory situations they may be confronted with. There is a wrong way and a right way to get such a sermon. The wrong way is to seek some intellectual platform for a collectively strategic philosophical approach. The right way, which is also the easy way, is for the preacher to prayerfully ask God for a message that speaks to every worshipper in the pew and be obedient to what He gives you. The latter is by far a better sermon every time.

B. Biblical Based

At the risk of sounding redundant, I just have to reiterate that the sermon must be based on the Scripture, the revealed word of God. I believe the mark of a good sermon is whether it preaches and lifts up the Name of Christ -- the grace of God, the love of God, the saving power of the blood of Jesus. There is nothing that can really substitute the Holy Scriptures. Too many sermons these days lift the name of John Wesley more than Jesus' name. I am not sure even John Wesley would like that.

The Word is more powerful than any other kind of knowledge we would care to share. Share it with all the power and know-how you have -- but more importantly, ask the Holy Spirit to guide and feed you on the truth that saves lives into eternity. By the way there are various "Translations and Versions " of the Bible today; one is free to choose the version that one is most comfortable with and is simple to comprehend, but the Word of God is one.

Finally, it needs to be mentioned that "scripture reading" is also an effective sermon. So it is important that the Bible is read out loud and clearly. The sermon one preaches is at best a commentary on the Word of God. If one had to make the choice between "reading the Bible and preaching," I would suggest that the former is more important. Some congregations may already be blessed to have someone who is naturally gifted in how to interpret the Word. If not, and if resources permit, it is worth considering sending a few people for a short course in oral interpretation. Their performance in reading the Bible will enhance your sermons markedly and ultimately your mission.

C. Action Filled Repentance

The sermon must, in God's name, persuade, invite or demand repentance. Attack ugliness of sin and depravity. When John the Baptist, the forerunner of Jesus, started preaching in the desert of Judea in Israel, he cried: "Repent, for the kingdom of heaven is near " [Matt. 3:2]. Likewise Jesus, in His preaching, demanded: "the time has come.... the kingdom of God is near. Repent and believe the good news " [Mark 1:15]. Let me illustrate the critical action of repentance with a secular parabolic incident, which most Zimbabweans have heard me preach before.

About three years ago I bought a bull for my herd of cattle. I would have preferred to name it Africa but the herd-man had already named him Russia. The bull's behaviour shocked me. It went all over the place, following whichever herd had cows in heat. Since the Brahman weighed several tonnes, it more or less literally threw its weight around such that the herd-man had a hard time bringing it home from pastures at the end of the day**. Several times it had wandered off, plodding through village vegetable gardens and fields -- destroying crops. Once it was missing for several days: we eventually found it miles away. Furthermore, it looked fierce and mean. It did not like jumping into the dip tank with other cattle nor could anyone have the nerve to spray it to destroy ticks. Russia became the talk of Muziti, my village. Russia's behaviour puzzled and embarrassed me.

So I entertained various ways of disposing of the beast. Should I sell it or slaughter the troublesome and disobedient beast? I also thought of giving it away in order to maintain good relations with neighbours. How could I keep it from being such a menace in the community and among their herds? I could not simply do nothing. I was concerned for the safety of the herd-man and the village kids. I was also concerned for Russia *himself*: he could contract a tick borne disease. Yes, indeed, I was also concerned for my investment.

My father's eighty-six year old first cousin, Ernest Mapfunde, (now late) advised me to build a corral for it alone and never let it out. My initial thought was that this was an extreme measure. I thought it over and considered what was at stake. I followed this advice because it sounded reasonable. I made sure Russia was well fed inside the pen where it stayed 24 hours a day and seven days a week for about six months.

Finally one day I decided to release him to see if he would behave differently. I was delighted to discover the huge beast was completely reformed -- exhibiting totally different behaviour. The herd-man reported Russia was amenable to herding-instruction and was no longer a menace. Russia would come home from the pastures everyday with the rest of the herd. My neighbours were asking me (and are still asking) what we did to make-over Russia into a properly domesticated animal.

This got me thinking: if an animal could have a change of heart, i.e. if it could modify its behaviour, what more with human beings who were created in God's own image and have rational power?

We must continue to work with God to change the world, beginning with ourselves. The grace of God is made available to us through Jesus Christ. *Why should we be enslaved by our own habits? Why? One thing is certain; people will not change if no one preaches repentance to them. So, preach brother, preach... preach sister, preach. Proclaim Jesus' name.* God has invested the gospel with us: we must pass it on to the next generation, so preach.

A good evangelistic sermon usually leads people to change, and it also inspires them to seek God and His righteousness. It gives hope and courage. People can become reconciled to God and to each other, whether in family or in society, if they have heard the word and repented. A good evangelistic sermon touches not only the emotions, but the brain as well. Yes, emotions too. If soccer, football and baseball games can touch people emotionally , both old and young, why can't such emotions be touched by God's word, which addresses issues of life and death? Again we agree with Dr Alan Walker when he says,

"True preaching seeks to present a case convincingly in an effort to win the mind of the hearer. But intellectual argument without the fire of emotions often leaves men as they are " (Walker, 1980,99).

D. No Censorship in God's Business

God's message to the individual is never abridged. Why should the preacher attempt to screen God's message to God's own people? I sincerely believe that the message that God gives to the preacher as a result of prayer, *must be preached as it is.* Some preachers are tempted to preach what people want to hear, rather than what people need to hear. I contend that when God gives a prophetic message, let it be so. *To change it is not only cowardice but also disobedience to the Holy Spirit who commissions the prophet. Worse still, altering God's word to His people who are seeking God's word, is cheating the worshippers -- wasting their time and leading them to death rather than resurrection.*

I understand that in some churches in the USA, one of the main reasons for treating Jesus and the Holy Spirit as museum pieces or religious souvenirs, and shun talking about spiritual rebirth, is that the majority of the pastors in such churches are "slaves" of their own congregations. The pastors have long been denied their freedom in the pulpit to preach the truth that sets the people free. They must preach what the congregation wants them to, or else, either they are fired or some members leave. What a sad state of affairs, to make this choice. For them to preach Christ, might mean losing the "almighty dollar." They can only secure the "almighty dollar" when they preach "fish stories".

Of course there are exceptions to this general trend. Since effective evangelism decolonizes the soul, as I have defined the term in chapter four, then I believe the preacher should feel that he or she is under obligation to deliver God's people from their individual, self-imposed jail cells. Salvation is liberation. The sermon is expected to set the sin-sick souls free to be what God intended for them

E. Communicate

An evangelistic sermon must inspire and challenge the congregation so that they want to witness and share both the gospel and material things with the needy outside and in their church. In other words, the sermon should motivate them to action. This is achieved through relevance in your sermon.

Plan to use imaginative illustrations that are likely to draw the attention of the greatest number. Most preachers are aware that a "sermon without illustration is like a house without windows." Aim to be understood by using vivid illustrations. Be simple and clear. I seriously doubt the wisdom of using some foreign words when preaching to congregations that do not speak that language. For example, using English to Shona people in Zimbabwe only serves to make the gospel "foreign" rather than incarnate and even indigenous. It certainly makes some people uncomfortable, even angry, and why not? Worse still it deprives some of hearing the Word. One does not inspire people by talking "above them" or seeming to despise and underestimate them. This is partly why St. Paul discouraged the Asian churches from making a big deal out of speaking in tongues, like it is status. Of course in prayer, one can speak in tongues because he or she is "talking to God," but a preacher needs to communicate with the congregation in their own language.

The sermon must focus on where the people are. As Alan Walker says, "...the real battle which evangelism must win is the struggle for relevance. Bread and butter questions, down to earth themes, a language that is understandable, metaphors and illustrations which arise out of today's world. These are among the supreme needs of evangelism" (Walker, 1980,61). These are the ingredients of an effective evangelistic sermon. A relevant sermon is one that brings the word of God to the people of God in such a way that each one feels that God is speaking to him or her -- whether the word be condemnation or admonition, that does not matter. The important thing is for the hearer to feel: *God has spoken to me today.*

Relevance applies to every form of communication that must persuade humans to act. For instance in sub Sahara Africa, which has the highest statistics of people living with HIV, Behaviour Change Communicators are battling to design advertisements with relevance to specific target groups so that they go for voluntary HIV testing. The spread of the virus will continue unabated until people appreciate that these messages are meant for them. Likewise an effective evangelistic sermon must be contextual, and address local needs as well as specific concerns and individual's issues. When the Holy Spirit has inspired everyone in a sermon, the congregation must feel that the sermon is intended for him or her individually -- not for other people. To accomplish this, the preacher must ask God, in prayer, for inspiration. As already pointed out above, inspired messages are always relevant because God knows the aspirations of our hearts.

F. The A.B.C. of Sermon Delivery

Before you deliver the sermon you have so painstakingly prepared, you *must* rehearse several times in your bedroom, office or in the bush, imagining that the congregation is before you. This is the secret behind good sermon delivery. Some preachers call this rehearsal stage of preparation, *'Preaching to the pews/benches.'* Rehearse/Preach it many times over until you feel like you own it and it is part of your spirit. That way you will need little or no notes at all during delivery. I do not know about you, my experience has been that extemporaneous sermons[19] tend to be more inspiring and less rigid and formal. A preacher who gets glued to his or her manuscript will soon or later lose the audience's interest.

The actual sermon delivery calls for a few but very important steps:
Beware of spiritual "leakage", i.e. talking a lot before you ascend the pulpit. The preacher should not mingle too much with people immediately prior to delivery. Passing jokes and laughing around punches holes through your inspired

---

[19] Thoroughly prepared but delivered without notes.

sermon. Also, it creates the danger that some parishioners may think that you are talking about them should there be coincidence on the topic.

The best sermon aid you have is yourself: your character, reputation, sincerity as we pointed out earlier. Your relationship with the parish is what they see, before you even open your mouth. That is a frightening challenge for all of us preachers. Is it not?

The preacher's appearance can either distract the audience's attention or reinforce the message. Therefore *the preacher must adorn himself or herself appropriately.* This includes clothing items. By the way, wearing the pulpit robe is not trying to be more formal. The robe is intended to give simple appearance as the parishioners get accustomed to seeing their preacher wearing it. It must also add an earnest appearance associated with holiness.

Respect the audience, and let only the Scriptures/sermon speak to them, or even lead them to judge themselves. Furthermore, it is best to *avoid using the pulpit to fight your battles* (should there be any) with parishioners. Too many preachers, especially in Africa, preach sermons that sound like judges delivering high court sentences. Where are the sermons that teach God's love, mercy and grace? Let me remind them, yours is to deliver the inspired sermon: let the Holy Spirit convict them.

VI. HOPE FOR UNIVERSAL REVITALIZATION

In discussing the topic Pastor is Key, we should be careful not to create the false impression that God is not involved. There is hope! As we pointed out in Chapter 2. God will not let His church die. If it does die, I am sure God will find another way to "revive us again." God could bless us with another Pentecost experience we read about in Acts, Chapter 2; or what happened in the Zimbabwe Church in 1918 at Old Mutare Mission Centre as we have discussed in Chapter Three. That is the hope for which we must pray with intensity, patience and trepidation.

There is hope, and when this is realized we will see its fruits in the pulpits of the churches that are currently declining, wherever they may be. When the time comes for desired changes to happen, transformation will begin with: seminaries, the pastor, revivalism, a new message, a new person and a resurrected church!

The Seminaries and Theological Colleges

Some seminaries and theological colleges will have to be transformed from being spiritual slaughter houses to being centres of spiritual rejuvenation and empowerment -- Pentecostal centres. When that time comes, these institutions will produce pastors with "strangely warmed" hearts and not the spiritually DOAFS pastors we are receiving from some seminaries and colleges these days. I know there will be a lot of frowning and anger because of this statement. May I humbly suggest that when you calm down, look around ... notice how the Pentecostal Churches are thriving and mushrooming around us --often just next door to us. Then look again at Table 2 in this chapter. Do you know why? Why is there a difference? They are spirit-filled and led. They emphasize spiritual vitality. They believe and preach Jesus Christ, Holy Spirit, new birth and prayer -- nothing more, nothing less.

The Pastor
Is it absolutely necessary to have a born again pastor? Yes! Jesus ordered it (John 3:3).

Spiritual rebirth was not Nicodemus' idea. Rather, it was Jesus who said that rebirth must occur in order for one to see God's Kingdom. It is not Peter, Paul, the Pope of Rome, John Wesley but Jesus Christ who ordered it. The pastor must be filled with the Holy Spirit as Jesus promised (Acts 1:8). The pastor must be a person of prayer. Jesus said so: "Watch and pray" (Matt. 26:41). Suffice to say the *pastor will need to be a courageous preacher, a prophet, a spiritual physician called to heal the sin-sick souls in partnership with Christ.*

VII. A NEW 21ST CENTURY MESSAGE IS DUE

God may send another John Wesley or other firebrand revivalists to spearhead another revival or great awakening. At least this is my deep desire and prayer! The type of revival that saved England when that nation had "reached its lowest ebb," is due wherever the churches are now dry -- operating like exclusive secular clubs -- whether it is in the so-called "third world" or in the West or East. A revival is due.

Preachers will have to preach the old message in a new way ... the message of salvation and rebirth. I repeat, as it was ordered by Jesus Christ, Himself, "I tell you the truth, no one can see the kingdom of God unless he/she is born again from above" (John 3:3). This alone will save the dry church. Like many, I am also a fan of John Wesley but we all know that he is not the Saviour. Let us remember that it is Jesus who caused John Wesley to be such an effective evangelist during his day. Those who emulate him must seek what he sought -- the Holy Spirit. We know he valued the Holy Spirit above all other things because this 5 feet 3 inches (1.6 m) tall man, who weighed only 120 pounds (54.6 kg) was the son of a priest of the High Church of England; he too became a priest in that same church; he had an M.A. degree from the prestigious Oxford University, where most great and highly notably scholars went: but all these came secondary to his own spiritual rebirth.

True, our social status and academic *summa cum laude* achievements are very, very good, and useful in the service of humanity. Go and get them. But they will not, I repeat, they will not qualify us to revive the church membership which is rapidly declining, on their own. What makes the difference is being born again, being filled with the Holy Spirit. I believe that the summa cum laude plus "strangely warmed hearts" is what it will take to effect spiritual renewal. The data in Table 2 clearly shows which groups are on the increase. A complete reversal has occurred. The older denominations are now trailing behind in growth rates. The first are now last -- the least! After considering everything we have presented in this book, look once more at that table and answer the question: *what has gone wrong?*

In sum, the Pastor is Key to congregational revitalization and resurrection by preaching rebirth. A Pastor with a vision to revitalize the congregation will have to be a spiritual giant along with being the shepherd and good administrator. In addition, we believe that it is the Holy Spirit who decolonizes souls that are ready to receive Him, after being led to the threshold of salvation by an evangelist -- you. Decolonized souls come together to form revitalized congregations that together restore denominations. The Holy Spirit is the power that drives the Key to function productively.

***

And now, I offer my solemn prayer for Africa (see Appendix 1) because I praise God that all the foregoing does not spell a hopeless situation. Yes, there is hope. God will not let His Church disappear; this, I know. He loves us too much to let that happen. In His own way, at His own time, God will revive us again as His people. He may create new denominations or He will restore our hunger and thirst for His righteousness. Hence we will seek Him earnestly, to be filled by Him, so that He can use us for evangelism that decolonizes the world by Holy Water and Holy Spirit. So the pastor must preach spiritual rebirth and spiritual baptism, since the main task of the pastor's preaching -- his or her primary duty, is to do so in the matrix of the Holy Spirit who revives the souls.

And now may the grace of our Lord Jesus Christ, the love of God and the fellowship of the Holy Spirit abide with you dear pastors/priests and all, now and forever. Amen.

ABOUT THE AUTHOR

Abel Tendekayi Muzorewa answered the call and went to seminary at Old Mutare Centre where he met and married Maggie Chigodora and became the *first couple* to wed in post dedicated Ehnes Memorial Church -- the same place he had accepted the Lord at the age of thirteen.

His abiding commitment to peace earned him awards from Pope John Paul II and the United Nations. In 1979, he became first black Prime Minister of Zimbabwe-Rhodesia, a position which ended prematurely. Retired from resident episcopacy of the United Methodist Church in 1991. Later he also retired from active political leadership. He is the current Patron of Araunah Mission Fellowship for visually impaired persons and still participates effectively in all worship services.

He holds a Diploma in Theology and a Bachelor of Arts degree in Religion and Philosophy from Central Methodist University; a Masters' degree in Ministry to Youth from Scarritte Bennette College; and several honorary Doctorates in Divinity, Human Letters and Laws.

***

The Bishop A. T. Muzorewa Evangelism Foundation was established in his honour (www.batmef.org). He now finds time and energy to do some poultry and vegetable farming at his rural cottage near Rusape, Zimbabwe. He is "retired but not tired,"

A Prayer for Africa

THE SCRIPTURE:

> *"The wolf will live with the lamb, the leopard will lie with the goat, the calf and the lion and the yearling together; and a little child will lead them. The cow will feed with the bear, their young will lie together, and the lion will eat straw like the ox. The infant will play near the hole of a cobra, and the young child put his hand into the viper's nest. They will neither harm nor destroy on all my holy mountain. For the earth will be full of the knowledge of the Lord as the waters cover the sea"* (Is. 11:6-9).

The prophet Isaiah here paints a dream picture of perfect peace, amazing peace, a form of prayer of hope for peace for Israel. Such is the dream and hope for peace for Africa that I desire from the depths of my soul. Therefore, I pour my soul unto the Lord in my prayer.

THE CONFESSION:
O Holy Spirit, who is God, Creator of the universe, the God who has always been. One who is, and shall always be, Almighty God, father of the Risen Lord Jesus Christ.
God the only Creator of humanity. We confess that we have not loved you with all our heart, soul, and mind (Matt. 22:37). And we have not obeyed your commandments to worship one God, and to love our neighbour as ourselves. We have committed the sin of worshipping other cultures; the sin of despising ourselves as black people. As a consequence of our disobedience of these greatest commandments which you gave us, we have lived under the power of the nature of evil; we have created the gods of greed, jealousy and idleness. We have actually destroyed ourselves by self-hate, wars, massacres, and hunger for power. That Africa has the greatest population of refugees, is clear evidence and verdict of our self-imposed oppression, in addition to foreign ideological oppression. The cry of the African people in Diaspora, scattered all over the world, is proof for self-imposed oppression and injustice. We lack moral, social and political integrity, yet we are created in your own image.

FORGIVENESS:
O Father God, we ask that through your unconditional love and your mercy, you forgive us and save us. Deliver us from the negative spirit of tribalism, witchcraft, sexism, male chauvinism, fear, superstition, war mongering, neo-colonialism and unjustified inferiority complex, and ignorance. Forgive us for saying "yes" when *"no"* is the truth; forgive us for cronyism and nepotism.

AFRICA'S SALVATION:
All these things we have mentioned as aspects of our self-destruction are only symptoms of hearts that are wicked. The root of all this is sin, defiled minds, and disoriented thinking. Therefore we pray that You, our Lord Jesus, the Lamb of God that uproots sin from the human heart, save us. Africa needs to be baptized with the spirit of truth.
We need the total cleansing of our culture, yes, salvation! Father God, we need spiritual regeneration and You alone can do that for us, we pray. Father God, we pray, therefore that You raise this century's breed of born again, holy spirit filled preachers/evangelists, men and women who will lead Africa to live, work and prosper in the spirit of Christ -- the Prince of Peace and Saviour of all creation.

THE PRAYER FOR YOUTH:
Almighty God, the Biblical God of Daniel, Meshach, Abed-nego, Shadrach, Joseph in Egypt, Esther, and Mary, we ask you to raise upright youths like Steve Biko of South Africa, in Africa. We ask that they may grow, "in wisdom and stature, and in favour with God and men" as Jesus did (Luke 2:52). We pray for the youth because they are today's and tomorrow's church. We pray for God-fearing youth who will form national government leaders to run affairs of the state in righteousness, integrity and genuine freedom, liberty and democracy for Africa.

PRAYER FOR THOSE IN POSITION OF LEADERSHIP:
First and foremost, we pray for their good health, wisdom, and high sense of justice, such as you gave to King Solomon.
Mighty God, who empowered Moses to say, "Let my people go" (Ex. 7:16), we pray that You appoint rulers who will lead us from oppression and neo-colonial mentality.
Leaders who… "are capable, who fear God, are trustworthy, who hate dishonest gain … (Ex. 18:21). TRULY FEAR God with a Godly love. Leaders who earnestly desire with all their heart, with all their soul, and all their mind to create for Africa, genuine freedom, liberty and democracy. Leaders who will deliver Africa from the economic oppression and imbalance due mainly to mismanagement.
O God, how long, oh how long shall we live in this sort of fool's paradise? Oh Lord, when will Africans stop running away from their own leaders to settle in foreign countries where true liberty, freedom and human dignity is observed?
We cry to You God, to please save us from and provide us now, we pray, with more sons and daughters like Nelson Mandela and others.

A CHRISTIAN CONTINENT:
God the Holy Spirit, who has power to change things, we pray that Africa be a Christian continent, characterized with love for all peace loving people. Transformed brotherhood and sisterhood of all, both black and white who live in

Africa. We desire a continent where all spears, knob carries, guns and other war weapons will be in museums and national archives; where peace and unity, freedom and democracy will be the heart beat and spiritual engine of Africa. God banish the devil and order him: "Out of existence!" We just desire to live in a land of sweet liberty, freedom… true brothers and sisters in diversity characterized with loving and caring of each other. Halleluiah! Amen.

APPENDIX 1

The harvest is truly great universally. The world population will never stand still. Therefore, the evangelists should never stop evangelising because more and more souls who are born every second need to be *born again* if they are to live eternally.

STATISTICS:

THE WORLD AT LARGE

World Population: 6 070 581 thousand from United Nations Population Division

Christians	2 Billion or 33 %
Non-Christians	4 Billion or 67%
SOURCE:	http://www.adherents.com/Religions_By_Adherents.html [Last modified 6th September 2002]

ZIMBABWE'S POPULATION

Population:	12.85 million [2001]
Race:	96% African
Ethnicity:	[Shona 82%, Ndebele 14%, Asian and white 4%]
Religion: &	50% subscribes to Syncretic [practice both Christian indigenous]
Christian:	26%
Traditionalist:	23%
Muslim and others:	1%

GEOGRAPHY

➢ Africa geographically occupies the combined landmass of China, India, Europe, Argentina, New Zealand, the continental United States and then more.
➢ Africa covers nearly 12 million square miles (31 million sq. km).
  The population was estimated at 795 million; percentage of African youth is 20.4%.   [According to the United Nations Population Division, 2000]

BIBLIOGRAPHY

Abraham, William J. *Logic of Evangelism*. Grand Rapids: Wm B Eerdmans Publishing Co., 1996.

Aristotle. *The Ethics of Aristotle, the Necomachean Ethics*. New York:Viking Press, 1980.

Armstrong, Richard Stol. *Service Evangelism*. Kentucky: Louisville: Westminister John Knox Press, 1979.

Barna, George. *Evangelism That Works*. Ventura: Regal Books, 1995.

De Jong, Peter Y. *Taking Heed to the Flock: A Study of the Principles and Practice of Family Visitation*. Eugene: Wipf and Stock Publishers, 2003.

Graham, Billy. *Death And The Life After*. Nashville: W Publishing Group, 1988.

- - - . *The Holy Spirit*. Nashville: Thomas Nelson Inc., 1978.

Hunter, George G., III. *To Spread the Power*. Nashville: Abingdon Press, 1987.

Idowu, E. Bolaji. *Olodumare: God in Yoruba Belief*. New York: Wazobia, 1994.

Job, Reuben P. *Issue One: Evangelism*. Nashville: Tidings, 1970.

Johnson, Samuel and Roger Mueller. *Selected Writing of Samuel Johnson*. London: Falcon Press, 1949.

Jones, Scott J. *The Evangelistic Love of God and Neighbour: A Theology of Witness and Discipleship*. Nashville: Abingdon Press, 2003.

MacDonald, William. *True Discipleship*. Ontario: Gospel Folio Press, (1936), 2003.

McGavran, Donald A. *Effective Evangelism: A Theological Mandate*. Phillipsburg: Presbyterian and Reformed Publishing, 1988.

Morris, George E. and H. Eddie Fox. *Faith-Sharing,* Nashville: Discipleship Resources, 1986.

Muzorewa, Gwinyai H. *The Great Being: Yahweh, Allah, God*. Eugene: Wipf and Stock, 2004.

Nelson-Pallmeyer, Jack. *Jesus Against Christianity*. Harrisburg: Trinity Press International, 2001.

Nhiwatiwa, Eben K. *The Humble Beginnings*. No data.

Roberts, W. Dayton. *Revolution in Evangelism: Evangelism-in-Depth in Latin America*. London: Billings and Sons Ltd., 1980.

Torrey, Reuben A. *How to Bring Men to Christ*. Chicago: Fleming H Revell Co., 1980.

Trumbell, Charles G. *Taking Men Alive*. New York: Fleming H. Revell Company, 1938.

United Methodist Church. *The Book of Discipline of United Methodist Church 2004*. Nashville: United Methodist Publishing House, 2004. (Selected lines from Part II)

Walker, Alan. *Evangelist Preaching*. Grand Rapids: Francis Asbury Press, 1988.

Hymns:
- Excerpts from hymns Murapi Aripano (108), Tora Zita Rake Jesu (188) and Tsitsi Dzinoshamisa (178) are from *Ngoma dzeUnited Methodist Church yeZimbabwe,* © United Methodist Conference Board of Publications and Communications, 1964.
- Excerpts from hymn Amazing Grace (92) is from *The Book of Hymns of the United Methodist Church*, ©1964, 1966 by Board of Publication of the United Methodist Church, Inc. USA.

Websites:
- www.adherents.com/Religions_By_Adherents.html
- www.africau.edu/about/structure.htm

www.ingramcontent.com/pod-product-compliance
Lightning Source LLC
Chambersburg PA
CBHW072151160426
43197CB00012B/2336